New Jersey's Civil War Odyssey

An Anthology of Civil War Tales from 1850 to 1961

Untold and Long-Forgotten Stories of New Jerseyans and How They Coped With the American Civil War and Its Memory, Including Accounts of New Jersey Civil War Political Myths, Jewish Jerseymen in the Ranks, A Confederate General From Elizabeth, Holding the Line at Gettysburg, Wartime Base Ball, the Hoboken Bounty-Jumper Sting, the "Great Reunion" at Deckertown, Strange Tales of War Monuments, a National Cemetery Full of Confederates, the Centennial Commission's Principled Stand Against Racism, and Much More...

Edited by
Joseph G. Bilby

New Jersey Goes to War:
Biographies of 150 New Jerseyans Caught Up in the Struggle of the Civil War, including Soldiers, Civilians, Men, Women, Heroes, Scoundrels — and a Heroic Horse.

A must-read for anyone interested in the history of the Civil War and noteworthy New Jerseyans who participated.

$20 plus $5 shipping and handling

Discover Your Community's Civil War Heritage
Discover the role of your town in the most significant even in American History - the great Civil War that determined whether our country would survive as a free and united country

A researcher's and genealogist's resource guide of researching Civil War veterans in your town.

$10 plus $5 shipping and handling

"Freedom to All"
New Jersey's African-American Civil War Soldiers

The definitive story of the New Jersey's black soldiers in the Civil War. This book also addresses African-American military service in New Jersey before and after the conflict, from Revolutionary War militiamen to the state's segregated First Separate Militia Battalion of the 1930s and the post-World War II New Jersey National Guard, which, in 1948, led the nation in integrating its military force.

$20 plus $5 shipping and handling

Copies are available online at: bit.ly/NJCWHA_Store
Order from Longstreet House, PO Box - 730, Hightstown, NJ 08520

Learn about new books that will be offered during the Sesquicentennial
Sign up for our Email Newsletter at: bit.ly/NJCW150_Contact

New Jersey's Civil War Odyssey

An Anthology of Civil War Tales from 1850 to 1961

Untold and Long-Forgotten Stories of New Jerseyans and How They Coped With the American Civil War and Its Memory, Including Accounts of New Jersey Civil War Political Myths, Jewish Jerseymen in the Ranks, A Confederate General From Elizabeth, Holding the Line at Gettysburg, Wartime Base Ball, the Hoboken Bounty-Jumper Sting, the "Great Reunion" at Deckertown, Strange Tales of War Monuments, a National Cemetery Full of Confederates, the Centennial Commission's Principled Stand Against Racism, and Much More...

Edited by
Joseph G. Bilby

An Official Publication of the New Jersey Civil War Heritage Association Sesquicentennial Committee

Printed by Longstreet House
PO Box 730, Hightstown, NJ 08520
www.Longstreethouse.com

Published by New Jersey Civil War Heritage Association
PO Box 442
Wood-Ridge, NJ 07075-0442
njcivilwar150.org

ISBN 978-0-944413-78-4

Introduction

About two and one-half years ago a few members of New Jersey's Civil War community met at East Jersey Olde Towne Village in Piscataway, New Jersey, for an initial discussion of the upcoming 150th anniversary of the Civil War. Our goal was to determine how to best observe and commemorate our state's important role in the watershed events of 1861-65. The outlook was not favorable. Legislation about a national sesquicentennial commission was, and is, bogged down in the legislative process in Washington. Back home in New Jersey, any potential government interest was hamstrung by the state's financial problems.

After careful consideration, our group decided to launch an all-volunteer effort funded solely by contributions and revenue from our own projects. Named the New Jersey Civil War 150th Anniversary Committee, the group functions as a committee of the New Jersey Civil War Heritage Association, which graciously allowed us to operate within their organizational structure. While not an official state commission, two governors and both houses of the New Jersey state legislature have endorsed the committee's work.

Our first project was *New Jersey Goes to War*, an anthology of 150 short biographies of 150 notable New Jerseyans from the Civil War era. The book has been a big success, both critically and as a source of funding for future projects. We are especially proud that *The Civil War News* cited *New Jersey Goes to War* as worthy of emulation by other state sesquicentennial organizations. Everyone who worked on the project donated their time and talent.

The committee is pleased to now publish *New Jersey's Civil War Odyssey*, which is, in effect, a companion volume to *New Jersey Goes to War*. This work presents a selection of New Jersey Civil War stories and three original poems ranging from the antebellum period to the work of the New Jersey Civil War Centennial Commission. Once again, all of the contributors have donated their services. Special thanks to Joseph G. Bilby, Henry F. Ballone, Thomas R. Burke, Steven D. Glazer, James M. Madden and Dr. David G. Martin, for their editing, writing, layout and publicity efforts as well as all of the other authors and everyone else who contributed to the project in any way. We believe this volume continues to bear witness to New Jersey's many contributions to this crucial era in American history.

John Zinn, Chairman, New Jersey Civil War 150 Committee

Editor's Note

The father of the New Jersey history "story" would have to be Frank Stockton. Although it did not touch on the Civil War, his book, *Stories of New Jersey*, initially published in 1896, was required reading in New Jersey schools for a generation or more (my well-worn copy was once the property of the Rahway "Department of Public Instruction"). Stockton's rousing tales, although they played somewhat fast and loose with historical truth as we know it today, set a precedent for other, more careful, future storytellers.

Those who came after Stockton established a high standard of excellence. Camden reporter Henry Charlton Beck, who set out to track down the legends of the Pine Barrens in the Depression years, developed into more than a pursuer of folktales, significant in their own right, and drew the attention of New Jerseyans of another generation to the fascinating human interest stories lurking along the state's forgotten byways.

John Cunningham, perhaps the most well-known raconteur of all things Jersey for the past sixty years, first as a feature writer for the long-gone and sorely missed *Newark News* and then as book author, brought the New Jersey history story to an ever wider public. It was Cunningham's series on New Jerseyans at war in the *News* at the time of the Civil War centennial that awakened an interest in both New Jersey and Civil War history in the editor of this work.

Thomas Fleming did not make a career of pursuing the New Jersey history short story. However, his accounts of the state's rich past (which he experienced in person growing up in Frank Hague's Jersey City) have been informed by a novelist's vivid prose and sense of character, making him a leading chronicler of the New Jersey narrative as well.

Marc Mappen, with his former *New York Times* series *Jerseyana* and book of the same name, as well as his more recent work *There is More to New Jersey than Just the Sopranos*, has carried the tradition of the New Jersey history "story" to new heights. *Jerseyana* provided the inspiration for the sesquicentennial series of books, of which this is the second installment.

We at the New Jersey Civil War Sesquicentennial Committee view this volume, then, as an homage to those who came before, to Stockton (with a caveat), Beck, Cunningham, Fleming and Mappen and, to paraphrase Jim Stephens, deputy director of Cape May's Historic Cold Spring Village, as an opportunity to carry on the serious business of enlightening and at the same time entertaining New Jersey readers and all those who enjoy stories of the roles played by ordinary folks in great events.

To that end, the contributors to this volume bring little-known and long-forgotten tales of New Jersey's people and their Civil War experience over a hundred-year period to light, from a stop on the Underground Railroad to the 1961 centennial commission's attempt, in an almost equally turbulent era, to commemorate the state's role in saving the Union. As in our first volume, *New Jersey Goes to War*, sources for further study are briefly noted at the conclusion of each essay, with more information in the bibliography. Come join us, then, on a journey into the twilight of historical memory.

Joseph G. Bilby, Editor
Wall Township, NJ
January 2011

Table of Contents

Veterans' Tales

Hope, NJ - the Hopkins' Place
by
S. Thomas Summers

Hopkins in his GAR veteran uniform
many years after the war. (John Kuhl)

A stop on New Jersey's Underground Railroad

Daddy tended to the black folk at night.
I'd hear him from my room cooking ham,
scrambling eggs. He wanted their bellies
to be heavy and warm. That way, he'd say,

sleep wasn't as scarce as it could be.
First time he called me to help, I was ten.
Daddy charged me with a cup of milk.
I was to serve it to a black boy

a tad younger than I was. When I saw him,
he was sitting on the barn floor, back up
against the wall. I kinda felt like he wanted
to slide himself into the wood he was leaning on,

forget what he was, forget he was running,
just be a part of the wood's grain –
something everyone saw, but never cared
to bother with. I stretched my hand out,

offered him the milk. He didn't take it like I thought
he would. He just stared up at me – the whites
of his eyes as white as the milk I wanted him to drink.
And his eyes were big, so big I believed he could

see Jesus talking with God way up in heaven.
Now, he never took the milk. Daddy told me
just to leave it, so I set the cup at his feet.
I told him good luck and turned back for the house.

Before I got out the barn, I heard him say to me,
You find some luck ya'self. That night, I believe I did.

(An older Charles Hopkins went on to put his life on the line for his abolitionist beliefs. He was awarded the Medal of Honor for actions at Gaines' Mill and later survived Andersonville Prison Camp.)

Violence at the Edge of a World
The Battle of Pine Swamp
by
John G. Bilby

Early nineteenth-century free African-American communities in southern New Jersey were self-sustaining worlds unto themselves, societies that relied upon nearby Quaker goodwill and an intense sense of shared self-reliance. Out of necessity, these communities forged identities as places of thrift, industry, personal discipline and responsible citizenship, for at the edge of their worlds lurked slave catchers seeking fresh blood and fugitives, and the slightest slip had repercussions beyond the individual, effectively shattering the community itself. Nowhere was this better illustrated than by the "Battle of Pine Swamp," a violent community uprising in defense of a single man in a diverse settlement two miles south of Mount Holly named "Timbuctoo," after the ancient African center of learning.

Free blacks in the United States faced a challenging and often dismal existence in the years prior to the Civil War, as their universe of opportunities and possibilities steadily contracted. By the time the conflict began, there were roughly a half-million free people of color in the country, with half of them living in Southern slave states. Free African-Americans had benefited economically from the shrinking of the slave labor force in the early part of the nineteenth century by taking on paid work as field hands during harvest seasons; the shortage of labor meant that there was no racial animosity between workers, with many slaveholders going so far as to "[praise] the free Negro's industry, sobriety, and loyalty and [ask] that he be left alone." Rural communities were self-supporting, although necessarily a part of the white agricultural industry as well. This world shrank, however, as the post-revolutionary liberalism of the turn of the century hardened into a Southern conception of a planters' republic run by the slave-owning gentry for the benefit of poor whites. This development pushed many free blacks out of the South. After all, they had no place in this developing worldview, and they came to be viewed as threatening to the slaveholder as well as to the poor whites who had briefly labored alongside them. By the 1850s, some states had passed laws that invited free blacks to virtually enslave themselves, which some of them did, a testament to the effectiveness of the economic restrictions placed upon free people of color in the antebellum years.

If free blacks threatened the economic security of laboring whites with their sense of industry, they disturbed the slave system by their mere presence; slaveholders blamed them for corrupting their slaves with the seditious idea of freedom, not to mention the fact that their existence gave slaves a model to aspire to. Legal action against manumission and the status of free blacks following slave revolts serves as evidence of this punitive stance, driven by suspicions in the white community. Such concerns were a result not only of the intermingling of slave and free communities, but the fact that "blacks constituted an intimate part of the general community." Although free blacks in the South did not engage in potentially deadly protest, they refused to swear allegiance to the planter class and instead constructed self-reliant communities. These closed communities would become worlds unto themselves in the free black settlements in southern New Jersey as well, and would be so vital to their inhabitants' sense of self that they would kill to defend them.

When New Jersey African-Americans armed themselves to resist, slave catchers often ran into more than they bargained for. (Dennis Rizzo)

Residents of the southern New Jersey communities understood that their race made them subject to the whims of slave catchers, whether they harbored fugitives or not. Communication between New Jersey's free black communities and slaves in the states of the upper South was limited but growing, thanks to the state's numerous waterways, as well as the industrial expansion of shipping in the region: "Free black boatmen and stevedores helped slaves and their families aboard ships bound for Philadelphia and other ports." One slave famously escaped by boxing himself and shipping himself to a northern address.

Springtown, a historically black community in Cumberland County, set slightly off the Delaware Bay by the city of Bridgeton, began as a slave refuge at the turn of the nineteenth century. The town's ease of access for fugitive slaves, however, cut both ways; for example, the harassment of slave catchers drove the family of Samuel Ward farther north towards the end of the 1820s. Ward recalled that: "So numerous and alarming were the depredations of kidnapping and slave-catching in the neighborhood, that my parents, after keeping the house armed night after night, determined to remove to a place of greater distance and greater safety." The threat of re-enslavement did not, however, threaten the community's existence; instead, it hardened the resolve of those who remained. Springtown comes across as an armed camp in one narrative: "Free people were always armed with their old flintlock muskets, ready to kill and slay their enemies at any time. In fact, Springtown had their watchmen, and every strange white man had to give a good account of himself or leave." The residents of free black communities in southern New Jersey understood the peculiar precariousness of their situation: they were a refuge of easy access from points south, and it was necessary for them to be armed and on guard in anticipation of raids and reprisals by Southern slaveholders.

Swamp on the edge of Timbuctoo today. (Dennis Rizzo)

The lack of legal recourse or recognition of free communities of color by the state necessitated such an armed defense. Although there was an instance of the courts freeing blacks who had been captured by a slave catcher in Salem, it seems as though such instances were exceptions to the rule. The constant threat of re-enslavement in the region precipitated the violent defense of Timbuctoo in December 1860. The settlement's close proximity to Philadelphia, as well as its swampy terrain, made it a haven for fugitive slaves. One slave catcher from Philadelphia, a man by the name of George Alberti Jr., sought to capture Perry Simmons, who had been living peacefully in the community with his wife and children for over a decade. Alberti led a vigilante band into New Jersey in the attempt. A battle raged at the border of the community, at the edge of the village by Rancocas Creek. Several people were injured, and the slave catchers were driven off without their quarry. Simmons would die a little over a year later, allegedly never regaining his health after the bitterly cold night he had spent eluding Alberti's posse – *The New Jersey Mirror* remarked that "Perry is at last beyond the reach of his Southern master." Such a eulogy captured the grim reality of free African-American communities in southern New Jersey in the time leading up to the Civil War. Their existence was under constant threat from the encroachments of the Southern planters and their agents. In the face of a legal system that barely recognized their right to exist, armed resistance was the only rational choice. When the men of these communities gained the right to join the Union army and strike back at the slave power, they did so in droves. (Genovese, *Roll, Jordan, Roll*; Rizzo, *Parallel Communities; The Bold Defenders of Timbuctoo:* bit.ly/Timbuctoo)

Abraham Lincoln and New Jersey
by
Dr. David G. Martin

Lincoln's New Jersey Ancestry

It is not commonly known that President Abraham Lincoln had direct ancestors who lived in New Jersey. His great-grandfather, John Lincoln, was born in Freehold (then Monmouth Court House) in 1711, the son of Mordecai Lincoln and Hannah Salter. John Lincoln moved to Pennsylvania by 1740, and the president's grandfather, also named Abraham Lincoln, was born in the Keystone State in 1744. Abraham Lincoln the grandfather moved to Virginia, where the president's father, Thomas Lincoln, was born in 1780. Thomas moved to Kentucky, where he married Nancy Hanks in 1806, and President Abraham Lincoln was born there on February 12, 1809.

The president's great-great-grandmother, Hannah Salter, had an even closer connection to New Jersey. She was born in 1692 in Freehold, and her father, Richard Salter (the president's great-great-great grandfather), owned and operated Salter's Mill, located on today's Route 526 near Imlaystown. Hannah Salter married Mordecai Lincoln, the president's great-great-grandfather, in Freehold in 1714. Mordecai reportedly worked at Hannah's father's mill from about 1715 to 1720, prior to the family's move to Pennsylvania. Salter's Mill is now a National Historic Site. It was originally built in 1695, though the surviving structure is from a later date. A historical marker at the site reads: "Richard Salter owned this mill and an ironworks. Son-in-law, Mordecai Lincoln, was great-great grandfather of A. Lincoln."

Lincoln's only ancestral relative buried in New Jersey is Deborah Lincoln, a daughter of Mordecai and Hannah who was born in 1717 and died about 1720, and is buried in a small cemetery on Route 524 in Imlaystown. Deborah Lincoln was the future president's great-aunt.

Lincoln's Visits to New Jersey

Abraham Lincoln never spent a night in New Jersey. Nor did he ever campaign in New Jersey, either while seeking the Republican nomination or during his two presidential campaigns. He did, though, pass through the state several times while on his way between New York and Philadelphia and, on February 21, 1861, and June 24, 1862, stopped to deliver brief speeches.

Following his famous Cooper Union speech in New York City on February 27, 1860, Lincoln received invitations to speak in Paterson, Orange, and Newark, but declined them all, claiming that he was too worn out from his campaign swing through New England and New York. He returned to Illinois, where he received the Republican Party's nomination for president on May 18, 1860, at the party's Chicago convention.

Gutzon Borglum's seated Lincoln in front of the old county courthouse in Newark. (Henry F. Ballone)

After Lincoln won the election of 1860, New Jersey's Governor Charles Olden invited the president-elect to speak in Trenton while traveling to his March 4, 1861, inauguration in Washington and Lincoln agreed to the governor's request. Following two nights in New York City, Lincoln took the ferry to Jersey City on the morning of Thursday, February 21, 1861. He was greeted by numerous state and local dignitaries and thousands of citizens. After speaking a few words to the crowd, he ended with a typical lighthearted joke: "There appears to be a great desire to see more of me, and I can only say that from my position, especially when I look at the ladies in the gallery, I feel that I decidedly have the best of the bargain."

The president-elect spoke a few words at succeeding brief stops in Newark, Elizabeth, Rahway, New Brunswick and Princeton Junction, where he was serenaded by a large group of College of New Jersey (now Princeton University) students. (The college would award Lincoln an honorary doctoral degree in law in 1864.) Lincoln's train was greeted by a thirty-four gun salute when it arrived in Trenton about 12 noon. He then took a short carriage ride from the station to the state capitol. The carriage, property of Jamesburg businessman James Buckelew, was on display for many years in Trenton's City Museum. It was later returned to Jamesburg and has been fully restored by the Jamesburg Historical Association.

While the New Jersey State Senate awaited Lincoln's arrival, the following resolution was humorously considered: "Resolved: That we trust that this legislature may always have a Democratic member that shall exceed the President-elect by two and a half inches in height." Upon arrival at the senate, Lincoln was received courteously and delivered a short prepared speech. After alluding to New Jersey's important role in the Revolution, he reaffirmed his determination to preserve the Union. He then crossed over to the assembly chamber and delivered another speech, stating that he was devoted to peace but would put his foot down firmly if necessary, to which there was much applause.

After a brief lunch break, Lincoln made a few remarks to a crowd gathered outside the statehouse and then took the train to Philadelphia at 2:30 P.M., after spending just two and one-half hours in the state. Lincoln's second visit to New Jersey, on June 24, 1862, was even briefer. Returning from West Point after consulting with Winfield Scott, the former general-in-chief who had retired in October 1861, he stopped to deliver a short speech in Jersey City.

The president's final visit to New Jersey was a posthumous one. His body passed through the state as his funeral train traveled from Philadelphia to New York on Monday, April 24, 1865. The route was essentially the reverse of the one Lincoln had followed on his way to Washington in 1861. The train left Philadelphia about 4 A.M. and proceeded slowly, without stopping, through Trenton, Dean's Pond, Princeton, New Brunswick, Rahway, Elizabeth, and Newark, arriving in Jersey City at 10 A.M., when the presidential coffin was conveyed to a ferry for its trip across the Hudson to Manhattan. Public viewings were held in Philadelphia and New York City, but not in New Jersey. This trip through Jersey lasted a little less than six hours. In death, just as in life, Lincoln never spent a night in the state.

Mrs. Lincoln spent considerably more time in New Jersey than her husband. In August 1861, she and her two youngest sons, Willie and Tad, vacationed at Long Branch. Lincoln's personal secretary John Hay was with them and found the shore resort "hideously dull." Returning in the summer of 1863, Hay wrote that there was "disgusting bathing, pretty women." Mrs. Lincoln also reportedly vacationed later at Cape May.

The Presidential Elections of 1860 and 1864

In the 1860 presidential election, Lincoln lost the New Jersey popular vote with 58,346 votes out of 121,215 cast, though he ended up carrying four of the state's seven electoral votes due to a lack of coordination between his opponents, who tried at the last minute to run a "fusion ticket" to defeat Lincoln (electoral votes were assigned by congressional district, not "winner take all").

In the 1864 presidential election, New Jersey was one of only three states (the others were Delaware and Kentucky) to vote against Lincoln and in favor of the Democratic candidate, General George B. McClellan. The final popular vote was 68,020 for McClellan and 60,724 for Lincoln (who was actually running on the National Union ticket, not as a Republican). Lincoln lost all seven of the state's electoral votes.

Lincoln's Jersey Jokes

Perhaps because of his lack of electoral success in the state, Lincoln apparently never cared much for New Jersey. He had a few friends from Jersey, most notably former governor William Newell, with whom he had served in the U.S. Congress in the late 1840s. New Jerseyan William L. Dayton defeated Lincoln for the Republican vice presidential nomination in 1856. Joel Parker, the state's Democratic governor from 1863 to 1866, was a severe critic of the president, though he still generally supported Lincoln's war aims. Lincoln never appointed anyone from New Jersey to his cabinet.

Abraham Lincoln enjoyed telling jokes and stories to either convey a message or entertain. He told at least two about New Jersey. Once, when five important New Jersey politicians visited the president's office, he reportedly whispered to a friend, "The State of New Jersey is a long, narrow state. These men come from the north end. I should think, that when they left, it would have tipped the state up."

This second joke is more elaborate – and obscure. According to Lincoln, on one stormy night in December a ship was wrecked off the coast of New Jersey, and all aboard went down with the craft except one man. This sole survivor grabbed a floating spar and drifted toward the shore, where laborers from the Camden and Amboy Railroad gathered on the beach with ropes and boats. The Jerseyans threw him a rope and shouted, "You are saved! You are saved and must show the conductor your ticket!" The drowning stranger, however, resisted their efforts to haul him ashore and cried out in a weak voice, "Stop! Tell me where I am. What country is this?" When he heard the reply, "New Jersey!" the wretched stranger let go of the rope, exclaiming, "I guess I'll float on a little farther." And he was never seen again.

The joke would seem a dig at New Jersey, in that not even a drowning man would deign to land there. However, the joke's intent is complex because of the fact that Lincoln's friend, former Governor Newell, was responsible for the creation of the United States Life-Saving Service through the so-called "Newell Act" of 1848. In fact, Lincoln appointed Newell to the Life-Saving Service of New Jersey for a time during the Civil War. Perhaps the story was meant to reflect some kind of falling out between the two men. The mention of the Camden and Amboy Railroad, a monopoly widely regarded as overly expensive and unsafe, may also have been part of the story's rationale.

Lincoln Remembered

Lincoln the Mystic, **by James Earle Fraser, sits at the entrance of Hudson County's Lincoln Park, near the beginning of the Lincoln Highway. (Henry F. Ballone)**

Jersey jokes and bad election results to the contrary, New Jersey has remembered the sixteenth president and there are several notable Lincoln statues in the state, among them the seated Lincoln by Gutzon Borglum (1911) in front of the old county courthouse in Newark, another seated Lincoln, by James Earle Fraser in Jersey City's Lincoln Park, and "Lincoln the Rail Splitter," by Archimedes Giacomantonio (1987) at the Sparta Public Library ("Abraham Lincoln and New Jersey."; Zall, *Abe Lincoln Laughing;* bit.ly/LincolnClassRoom).

Lincoln and the *Ocean Emblem*
by
J. Mark Mutter

Abraham Lincoln never set foot in Toms River or Ocean County. The closest he ever came was Trenton, on his railroad journey throughout the Northern states to Washington, D. C. as president-elect in February 1861.

With the nation on the verge of a civil war, Lincoln's travels through the North quite purposely included New Jersey—even though he had failed to win all the state's electoral votes in the four-way election of 1860, a contest characterized as a "confused melee" in New Jersey by the *New York Times*.

Although he lost the state, Ocean County voters supported the president-elect by a wide margin. The *Ocean Emblem*, the county's then weekly newspaper, had supported Lincoln's candidacy with passionate editorials.

In an October 31, 1860, opinion column, entitled "Reasons for Doing Right," the *Emblem* declared:

> Why do we support Abraham Lincoln?
>
> There are various but those which refer more particularly to the man may be summed up as follows:
>
> He is honest. He is a friend of American labor. He is opposed to the extension of slavery. He is inflexibly opposed to corruption and intrigue in every form. He is a true representative of principles held by the fathers of the Constitution.
>
> These reasons appeal to the honest judgment of men. They are not to be disproved, and they form the only honest ground for supporting candidates for office.

Following the onset of war, that support was manifest across Ocean County as men rallied to the cause of the Union, almost 500 of them volunteering for service during the course of the conflict. They did their part to assure that the Union was saved and freedom and democracy survived—so, that in Lincoln's words, the government of the United States did not "perish from the Earth."

The *Ocean Emblem*, like other papers of the day, reported those immortal words delivered at the national cemetery in Gettysburg as a "short address by President Lincoln." The importance of the Gettysburg Address may have eluded the good editors of the *Emblem*, but it has sounded down the years as a manifestation of aspiration to the better angels in all of us. (*Ocean Emblem*)

Cranford and Abraham Lincoln
by
Steven D. Glazer

Although Abraham Lincoln spent little time in New Jersey, he nevertheless personally touched the lives of many living in the state. And the citizens of at least one Union County town, Cranford, may have had an unusual number of personal ties to the nation's Civil War president and his family.

One Cranford resident, William P. Westervelt, a telegraph pioneer, helped foil the first assassination plot again President-elect Lincoln as he made his way from Springfield, Illinois, to Washington, D. C., for his first inauguration. During the evening of February 22, 1861, Westervelt secretly cut the telegraph lines between Harrisburg and Maryland, preventing news of Lincoln's early departure by special nighttime train from reaching Baltimore, where would-be assassins were lying in wait.

Three Cranford townsmen were members of the 7th New York State Militia, the first full-strength regiment to safely arrive in Washington and protect the besieged president after his urgent call for Northern volunteers when Confederate artillery fired on Fort Sumter. The three men — Henry J. Phillips, Edward S. Crane and Thomas Elliott — were among those saluted by a relieved and smiling Lincoln as the regiment marched past the White House on April 25, 1861.

Reverend W. H. Roberts attended church services with the Lincoln family in Washington during the Civil War.
(*The Cranford Citizen*)

Another future Cranford resident, James Turnbull, was said to have shaken President Lincoln's hand shortly after his regiment fought at Bull Run, the first major battle of the Civil War. A major developer of Cranford, Henry R. Heath, was at the head of the line to shake the hand of the president as he greeted the first Union prisoners to be exchanged in the early days of the war. Heath had spent four months near death in Richmond's infamous prisons before a formal exchange was obtained by Lincoln.

A prominent clergyman in Cranford, Rev. William H. Roberts of the town's First Presbyterian Church, attended Sunday services during the war with Lincoln at the New York Avenue Church in Washington. Rev. Roberts, who often sat near the Lincoln family pew, would be cited frequently in later years for his firsthand accounts of the Lincolns' wartime religious practices.

An attorney who later settled in Cranford, La Roy S. Gove, attended Phillips Exeter Academy and Harvard College with the president's eldest son, Robert Todd. They were classmates and fellow members of the college's famous Hasty Pudding

Club. When Mrs. Lincoln and her youngest son Tad went to Cambridge, Massachusetts, in early summer of 1864, enjoying a brief respite from the war, they attended Harvard's graduation ceremonies and watched the two friends receive their diplomas.

And when the president and his wife attended a play at Ford's Theatre in Washington during the evening of Good Friday, April 14, 1865, a future town justice of Cranford, Wesley R. Batchelder, was there, too. He was then serving as confidential secretary to Union general Benjamin F. Butler. Years after President Lincoln was assassinated that night, Judge Batchelder would speak in town of the terrible events he had witnessed. James Turnbull, whose hand was shaken by

Henry R. Heath, the Cranford developer and former POW who shook Lincoln's hand. (Cranford Historical Society)

Lincoln in the first months of the war, later served in the honor guard that stood over the president's body as it lay in state at New York's City Hall, before continuing its mournful journey back to Springfield, Illinois.

Henry Heath, the Cranford developer who had been personally greeted by Lincoln after nearly dying in a Rebel prison, commemorated his wartime Commander in Chief by chairing the committee that erected the first overseas monument to him. In a driving rain in Edinburgh, Scotland, on August 21, 1893, Heath dedicated the bronze statue, *Lincoln Freeing a Slave*, to the memory of fallen Scottish-American soldiers. To this day, the statue remains the only foreign memorial to the men who fought and gave their lives in our country's Civil War. (Kline, *Baltimore Plot*; Styple, *Tell Me of Lincoln*; Swinton, *History of the Seventh Regiment*; *Lincoln Monument in Memory of Scottish-American Soldiers*)

John H. Margerum, "Princeton's Flag Man"
by
Robert F. MacAvoy

John H. Margerum as a captain in the 22nd New Jersey Volunteer Infantry. (NJ State Archives)

In 1861, just prior to the outbreak of the Civil War, the debate on secession at The College of New Jersey (today's Princeton University) rose to a fever pitch. At the time, no United States flag flew over the college or seminary campuses, and with about half the matriculating students from Southern states, a gesture like raising the flag would almost certainly be opposed by a significant portion of the student body. Despite this, an unknown individual raised a flag outside Nassau Hall, but it was soon officially taken down because it was unauthorized by the faculty, which was treading a fine line in an effort to discourage debate from escalating into potential physical confrontations.

John H. Margerum, a New Jersey Princeton student, disagreed vehemently with the college's official position and took it upon himself to right what he perceived as a grievous wrong. To the enthusiastic cheers of some of his classmates, who later presented him with a pair of revolvers for his daring, Margerum climbed the outside of Nassau Hall to the very top of the dome and tied a United States flag to the weathervane. The wind that day was blowing from the South so strongly that, with the weight of the newly attached flag, it bent the weathervane in a northerly direction, and it remained so throughout the war. Margerum had made his point. Following his feat, the faculty acquiesced and allowed the flag to float over the campus. Most of the Southern students subsequently returned home, many to fight in the Confederate army.

Margerum was no slacker himself. His patriotism and fervor persisted after the shooting started, and on September 2, 1862, he was commissioned a captain in Company G of the 22nd New Jersey Infantry, a nine-months regiment which, ironically, was a unit with a large number of reluctant Bergen County copperheads in its ranks. Margerum survived the war and died on June 4, 1904. He was buried in the Princeton Cemetery and a plaque next to his gravestone proclaims: "He risked his life by climbing to the dome of Nassau Hall to erect the stars and stripes of the Union Jack." (Hageman, *History of Princeton and its Institutions*; bit.ly/Margerum)

A marker at Margerum's gravesite commemorates his feat. (Diane C. MacAvoy)

"We will fight to the Death"
An Ocean County Volunteer Writes Home
by
J. Mark Mutter

New Jersey newspapers published letters from local soldiers throughout the war. In the absence of actual war correspondents, which few local papers could afford, these notes from the front brought the war to the home folks in an intensely personal way. One such letter, written from "Camp Keystone" in Washington, D. C., in September 1861 was published in Toms River's *Ocean Emblem*. The writer, Ocean County resident J[oseph] F. Thibeaudeau, was a private in "Halsted's Horse," a regiment later re-designated the 1st New Jersey Cavalry.

1st **New Jersey Cavalry monument at Gettysburg (Henry F. Ballone)**

Dear Emblem:— Last Saturday the rest of our Regiment arrived from Trenton, accompanied with Sergeant Irons of Tom's River, with nine more of little Ocean's gallant sons. Old Ocean is ever found on the side of the just and right, and is always ready and willing, both with men and money, to stand by this Union in its hour of need. All of us Ocean County boys return our heartfelt thanks to the patriotic and Union loving citizens of Tom's River.

If we ever get into an engagement you may expect to hear that the volunteers of Ocean did their full duty without flinching. We will fight to the death to restore this glorious Union of States, to its former splendor, and to re-unite the broken and scattered links into a perfect chain of peace, happiness, and prosperity.

I hope, and I think I will see before many months more, the glorious stars and stripes coming forth from the fiery ordeal through which it is now passing, purged of all dishonor, and with its broad stripes and bright stars floating in triumph and peace. "O'er the land of the free and the home of the brave."

It would not be months, but years, before the war would come to an end and Thibeaudeau, by then a battle-hardened sergeant in his second enlistment, would come home to, in his words, "peace, happiness and prosperity." By then, New Jersey had advanced from a state that Governor Charles Olden described in 1861 as "wholly unprepared," to an important cog in a successful war effort. (Jackson, *New Jerseyans in the Civil War; Ocean Emblem*)

War Comes to Westfield
by
Steven D. Glazer

More than 600,000 Americans under arms perished during the Civil War. And while many soldiers died in New Jersey of disease or wounds received on distant battlefields, no engagements between the North and South ever occurred on state soil. Nevertheless, at least one soldier from out of state met a horrific and bloody death in New Jersey.

The 2nd New Hampshire Volunteer Infantry Regiment was organized in Concord, the state's capital, in the spring of 1861. It was one of the early units formed in response to President Abraham Lincoln's call for volunteers. Company B, called the "Goodwin Rifles," was raised in the city by Charles Webster Walker, a 38-year-old native of Fryeburg, Maine. Walker, who in his youth apprenticed as a bookbinder in Concord — later serving as warden of Massachusetts State Prison — had recently returned to the capital, becoming engaged to a popular teacher there. He was widely considered one of Concord's most respected, intelligent and genial citizens. As a consequence, he was elected by the Goodwin Rifles to be their first lieutenant.

The 2nd New Hampshire — 1,000 strong — left Portsmouth, New Hampshire, on Thursday, June 20, 1861, for the seat of war. By Friday evening, the regiment had reached Elizabethport, New Jersey, where it disembarked from a steamboat and loaded onto rail cars of the New Jersey Central Railroad. Due to a lack of adequate rolling stock, the Goodwin Rifles' enlisted men were riding on open-platform cars, normally used for gravel, at the rear of the train. This left them exposed to the danger of being thrown off the train by sudden starts or stops, especially since no guard-rails had been provided on the cars. Also present at the train's rear was Lieutenant Walker, who had refused a place in the comfortably furnished passenger cars reserved for the regiment's officers, saying his duty was to ride with his men that night.

The train carrying the regiment moved slowly through Union County in the evening darkness. All along the way, despite the late hour, enthusiastic crowds of New Jersey citizens greeted the out-of-state soldiers, with ladies waving their handkerchiefs and well wishers frequently running up to shake the hands of the men.

Around midnight, as the train passed through the Westfield railroad station, Lieutenant Walker noticed that some of his soldiers were in an exposed position on the cars. As he rose and made his way among the men to warn them of the danger, an unexpected lurch threw the lieutenant under the wheels of the train, where his ankle and thigh were run over, almost completely severing the leg. By some accounts, Walker pleaded to be shot so as to end his misery. Instead, he was rushed to nearby Plainfield, where the regiment's surgeon — using the primitive techniques of the time — amputated the mutilated leg above the thigh.

Lieutenant Walker, after much suffering, died several hours after the operation, at 12:30 P.M. on Saturday. That Monday, *The New York Times* carried news of the lieutenant's death on its front-page.

Lieutenant Charles W. Walker was the first officer from New Hampshire to die in the Civil War. After his remains were returned to Concord, the entire city, as well as the state's government, closed down for a massive funeral. Four weeks later, Walker's regiment would be among the last to leave the battlefield at Bull Run, where it suffered more than 100 casualties.

Although Walker was only the first of 350 men to die while serving with the 2nd New Hampshire — one of the top fighting units in the Union army — it was reported that "no man in his regiment probably possessed better prospects for usefulness and promotion." In Westfield today, nothing remains to mark the place where this Granite State patriot fell. And his wartime tombstone in Concord's Old North Cemetery long ago mysteriously vanished. But perhaps during the sesquicentennial of the Civil War the memory of Lieutenant Walker will again be honored by those who have been reminded of his sacrifice for the Union. (Concord *New Hampshire Patriot*; Concord, New Hampshire, *Daily Independent Democrat*: *New York Times*; Haynes, *Second Regiment*)

> The Second New-Hampshire Regiment, Col. G Marston, arrived to-day at 2 o'clock, with full ranks, finely equipped, and bringing a complete band. Lieut. Chas. L Walker, of Concord, was accidentally killed by being knocked off the cars, in New-Jersey, near Plainfield. His leg was crushed and cut off by the cars, and he has since died. A train of cars came through direct from Jersey City via Easton, Harrisburgh, and Baltimore.

Initial account of Lieutenant Walker's death (with his middle initial incorrect) on the front page of the *New York Times* of Monday, June 24, 1861 *(New York Times)*

"He would do so again if ordered"
Archibald Gracie's Irrepressible Conflict
by
James M. Madden

Reflecting on New Jersey's role in the Civil War usually does not cause images of gray uniforms to come to mind. Several men born or raised in New Jersey had strong personal and economic ties to the South, however, including wives and substantial business interests. With a significant stake in the success of the newborn Confederate States of America, they sometimes served as officers in the Confederate army.

One such Rebel Jerseyman was Archibald Gracie III. Born in 1832 to a wealthy and prominent New York family with Huguenot antecedents, Gracie had a long, aristocratic pedigree. His grandfather and father were shipping magnates. And the family name endures today in Gracie Mansion, built by his namesake grandfather and the official residence of New York City's mayors.

**Brigadier General Archibald Gracie, CSA
(James M. Madden)**

The Gracie family was allied by marriage with the political and mercantile powerhouse King family; young Archibald's uncle Charles King was his father's business partner and he had cousins who served as Union officers during the Civil War, one of whom, Rufus King, Jr., was a Medal of Honor recipient. Gracie's uncle and Rufus' father, Brigadier General Rufus King, organized the Army of the Potomac's famed Iron Brigade.

Although born in New York, Gracie spent a significant portion of each year in Elizabeth, New Jersey, then a popular summer retreat. Following study in Germany, he received a West Point nomination through his uncle, Hudson County congressman James G. King. Gracie graduated fourteenth in his 1854 West Point class alongside other men who would make their mark in the Civil War, including George Washington Custis Lee, oldest son of Robert E Lee, Oliver Otis Howard, John Pegram, William Dorsey Pender and James Ewell Brown ("Jeb") Stuart.

Young Gracie served as a second lieutenant in the 5th United States Infantry on the frontier until 1856, when, following his father's wishes, he resigned to join the family firm and was placed in charge of an expanding cotton-brokerage business in Mobile, Alabama. He returned to New Jersey to marry Josephine Mayo, a Virginia girl then living at the Hampton Place mansion in Elizabeth with her uncle, Mexican War hero and general in chief of the United States Army, General Winfield Scott.

Following the wedding, Gracie returned to Mobile, where he joined the state militia as a captain in that city's Washington Light Infantry. On January 4, 1861, the governor of Alabama ordered the state militia to occupy the federal arsenal in Mount Vernon. Gracie led one of the four companies that captured the arsenal with no opposition, and six days later Alabama seceded from the Union. Local newspapers hailed Gracie's loyalty to Alabama, one editor opining, "Although not Southern by birth, he nobly espoused her cause, and placed himself on the side of right and justice."

With war on the horizon, Gracie traveled north to collect his family and their possessions in New Jersey, wrap up business dealings in New York City and visit his relatives for perhaps the final time before returning to Alabama. Word of his arrival in New Jersey reached the citizens of Elizabeth, who expressed mixed emotions. Some, friends of the Gracie family, suggested a militia guard of honor to meet him at the train station, while others, hearing of his role in capturing the federal arsenal and feeling he betrayed a government he had once taken an oath to protect, suggested a rougher greeting. On the evening of February 27, 1861, an indignant and rowdy "Black Republican" mob of more than 500 marched up to the Hampton Place home Gracie was then sharing with his in-laws. Angry Jerseyans filled the night with a cacophony of banging tin pans, blaring horns, singing and shouting. The unexpected commotion in a usually quiet, upscale neighborhood startled the Mayos, who threw open their windows to determine the cause of the uproar only to rapidly shutter them under a barrage of Roman candles.

The crowd settled down, and one of its leaders read aloud a proclamation calculated to speed Archibald Gracie on his way:

> Now, be it known, that we, the people of Elizabeth, with the firm determination on our part to resent the insult offered to our national flag by the cowardly traitor, do hereby, with a hearty good will, give him, the said Archibald Gracie, Jr, twenty-four hours' notice to evacuate the loyal city of Elizabeth, otherwise he will be donated a suit of clothing not set down in the programme - Vox Populi

The "suit of clothing" referred to was one of tar and feathers. After posting copies of the proclamation around Hampton Place and throughout the city of Elizabeth, the demonstrators reinforced their point by setting ablaze several barrels of pitch. They then strung up a straw effigy of Gracie, pinned with a placard reading "Traitor to his country," and torched it as well.

Fortunately for Gracie, he and his family had already left for New York in preparation for a return to Alabama. Rumors persisted, however, that he was planning to come back to Elizabeth, and an incensed group of citizens congregated at the train station and prepared to greet him, the "suit of clothing" on their mind.

Gracie's Hampton Place home, circa 1860, in Elizabeth, which was attacked by a pro-Union mob in 1861. (Mills, *Historic Houses of New Jersey*)

The Union County sheriff requested that two militia companies be sent to Elizabeth to control and disperse the crowd and avoid further trouble.

Gracie's father defended his son's conduct in the press, maintaining that he had no choice in seizing the arsenal, since as a militia captain he swore an oath of allegiance to Alabama and was just following orders from the governor as New Jersey militia officers would in a similar situation. The elder Gracie claimed his offspring did not volunteer to seize federal government property and did not boast of his exploit, merely stating that "he would do so again if ordered." According to his father, Gracie's visit to Elizabeth and New York was not meant to be provocative, but "to avoid any allusion to political matters during the very short stay here that his engagements at his home admitted of his making."

On returning to Alabama, Gracie rejoined his militia company, which was soon incorporated into the Confederate army's 3rd Alabama Infantry. Later that year, he was promoted major of the 11th Alabama. By early 1862, with his "government paid West Point education" providing valuable experience to his new country, Gracie organized and was appointed colonel of a new regiment, the 43rd Alabama Infantry, nicknamed "Gracie's Pride." Colonel Gracie was eventually promoted to brigadier general and assumed command of the brigade. He became

18

known for his personal courage on the battlefield, particularly at Chickamauga, and was wounded at the siege of Knoxville in December 1863.

On recovering from his wound, General Gracie was transferred to Virginia, where he led a brigade in the defense of Petersburg and Richmond. In May of 1864 his unit came up against the Jerseymen of the 9th New Jersey Infantry, a fact that the *New York Times* quickly picked up on, reporting in June 1864 that:

> Archibald Gracie, formerly a resident of Elizabeth, is now a General in the rebel army and that in the last battle south of Richmond, he opposed the Ninth New Jersey, one company of which is from Elizabeth. This fellow GRACIE, while still in Elizabeth City, made himself so obnoxious to the loyal sentiment of the place that he was threatened with punishment, and narrowly escaped receiving it.

When the 9th New Jersey's Lieutenant J. Madison Drake was captured at Drewry's Bluff by his brigade, Gracie, who knew Drake since their boyhood in Elizabeth, greeted the lieutenant by stating he was proud to be fighting Jerseymen. Reviled by his former neighbors, Gracie was celebrated by those he forsook them for. In November 1864 the *Richmond Examiner* proudly reported that troops under Gracie's command had captured forty-three Yankee prisoners on picket duty at Petersburg. According to the paper, the general dashed with his men into the Yankee lines, and the writer then used the event to characterize the federal army as somehow un-American, noting that "as usual the foreign element predominated in the mass, and the swell of the 'rich Celtick brogue' and 'the sweet German accent' sounded in chorus like the grunt of a drove of pigs."

General Gracie would not have long to savor his victory. In early December 1864, shortly after learning of the birth of his daughter and preparing to go on leave, he was observing the Union lines through a telescope from a Petersburg trench when a Union shell exploded in the position, instantly killing him, an aide and a nearby captain.

Three days later in New Jersey, Gracie's mother, unaware of her son's fate, passed away. Archibald Gracie was eulogized in the Southern press and by Francis O. Ticknor's poem, "Gracie of Alabama!" The Jerseyman gone south was initially buried at Petersburg, but soon after the war the family reinterred him in the family plot at Woodlawn Cemetery in the Bronx, New York, where "Gracie of Alabama" remains to this day. (*Macon Telegraph; New York Herald; New York Times;* Mills, *Historic Houses;* Abbott, *Walking the Berkshires;* Warner, *Generals in Gray*)

An Unexpected Tragedy
by
James M. Madden

While it may have been "all quiet along the Potomac" on the night of October 5, 1861, the sounds and sights of combat came home with a vengeance to northeastern New Jersey, where Mayor Edmund T. Carpenter of Hudson City was bayoneted, not by the enemy, but by Union soldiers

Mayor Carpenter had a significant civic career beginning in the early 1850s. He was elected as a Hudson County freeholder, served two terms in the state assembly and then as a judge of common pleas prior to being elected mayor of Hudson City for four successive one-year terms. Carpenter was also an affluent cattle broker and owner of Hudson City's Carpenter Hotel.

Born in Pleasantville, Westchester County, New York, in 1820, Carpenter moved to New York City at an early age and then across the river to Hudson City, part of modern Jersey City's Journal Square and Heights sections. A short ferry ride from Manhattan, Hudson City was an early commuter town for well-to-do New York businessmen.

The old federal arsenal in Hudson City (James M. Madden)

Hudson City's "Old Arsenal" was a deteriorating War of 1812 building with a large parade ground located on Bergen Hill, a bluff overlooking Manhattan. At the outbreak of the Civil War, the location proved convenient to train a volunteer unit before it left for Washington, and a detachment of German-speaking recruits under the command of Colonel Eugene A. Kozlay arrived there from New York in the summer of 1861. Kozlay, a former Hungarian army captain and late New York customhouse clerk, organized these men into the 54th New York Volunteer Infantry, also known as the *Schwarze Jäger* ("Black Hunter") or "Barney Rifles" (after Hiram Barney, a sponsor) regiment. The men of the 54th were issued a snappy uniform of green frock coat, gray pants and black cap, with green trim and a "death head" skull ornament on the cap.

After recruiting slowly through the summer, the 54th was finally mustered into the Union army for a three-year enlistment in the fall. The regiment's stay in Hudson City proved a tumultuous one, marked by quarreling among the officers and desertions among the men. Colonel Kozlay paid local saloonkeepers to supply his troops with beer to keep them happy, but apparently to no avail. Although some local merchants and taverns valued the regimental trade, several local women reported being accosted in the streets by inebriated soldiers from the 54th, easily identifiable by their green uniform coats.

Colonel Eugene Kozlay, 54th New York Infantry (USAMHI)

On the evening of Saturday, October 5, the regiment's increasingly troubled relationship with the community came to a head when a soldier walking down a street near the camp brushed against a young woman, Matilda Conk. Conk's husband Henry, walking a few yards behind her, interpreted the incident as an "indecent assault" and attacked the young German, continuing to beat him as he fled into a nearby store. The soldier finally broke free and stumbled back to the Old Arsenal, where his comrades immediately set out to avenge him, heading into the city in search of the Conk residence. Mistaking "Hank" Newkirk, a hotelier and saloonkeeper on the Five Corners, for "Hank" Conk, the mob assaulted Newkirk's establishment with a shower of bricks and debris, breaking windows and shutters and hitting a hotel patron reading a newspaper in the parlor in the head with a brick. The soldiers then charged into the hotel saloon and attempted to drag Newkirk into the street. The tavern's patrons intervened and ushered the hotel proprietor to safety behind closed and locked doors as the attackers withdrew to the Old Arsenal.

News of the attack traveled rapidly and, as fire bells rang throughout the city, a crowd of over 300 angry citizens gathered outside the hotel, ready to take revenge on the soldiers. News of an impending major riot traveled quickly back to the Old Arsenal as well, and Colonel Kozlay dispatched armed guards to round up all of his troops around the city and bring them back to camp. One of these squads encountered the outraged crowd gathering outside Newkirk's Hotel, and a confrontation immediately followed.

Mayor Carpenter, in an attempt to defuse the situation, positioned himself between the soldiers and civilians as both sides began to hurl insults and then advance on each other. Within an instant, Carpenter found himself in the middle of a maelstrom of pushing, shoving and swinging. One soldier armed with a camp hatchet was beaten to the ground by the mob but saved, ironically, by the Hudson City coroner. Several citizens were injured, among them the mayor, who was stabbed five or six times in his head and body by bayonets. Order was restored after the soldiers disengaged and successfully fell back to their camp, and the dangerously injured mayor was carried to his home. In expectation of more trouble, a number of special policemen were sworn in that night, and militiamen from Bergen and Hudson counties were placed on standby alert. The following day's newspapers reported the incident, and assessed Carpenter's injuries as mortal.

Colonel Kozlay agreed to hand over any soldiers involved in the incident to the local authorities and offered to pay for all damages incurred. There is, however, no indication that any soldiers were ever arrested or charged for the stabbing of the mayor. There were calls for a citizen attack on the Old Arsenal that never materialized, although one of the camp guards was struck in the head and slightly injured by a rock tossed by a civilian several nights after the riot.

Within the Old Arsenal the 54th continued its regular activities, including a previously scheduled ceremony where silk colors were presented to the regiment along with gifts to the officers. Perhaps as a peace gesture, Colonel Kozlay invited the general public, especially the citizens of Hudson City, to the event, publishing an advertisement in the newspapers. Interestingly, the invitation was carefully worded so that only couples were admitted – in Kozlay's language, "a gentleman and a lady" – no doubt because males in the company of females were less likely to cause trouble. Although the local militia was placed on alert, there were no difficulties. The occasion was peaceful, with music and dancing into the night until a steady rain broke up the festivities.

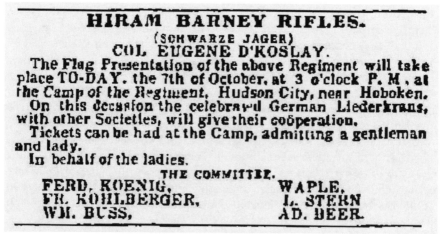

Announcement of the 54th's Flag Presentation (*New York Times*)

As the 54th New York celebrated, and made peace with at least some of the people of Hudson City, Mayor Carpenter's health was, according to the newspapers, improving, but he was still confined to his home. Deputy Mayor Garrett Van Ripher assumed the official public civic duties as acting mayor.

The 54th left the Old Arsenal and Hudson City for Washington on October 28. The riot seemed to fade from public memory, with no word of it in the media until Mayor Carpenter died of his wounds on Thanksgiving Day, from an internal infection and fever the physicians of the day were powerless to remedy.

Carpenter was laid out and waked at his home, as was the custom of the time. The funeral procession was over a mile long, and attended by many Hudson County dignitaries, elected officials and citizens. At the memorial service, Rev. Dr. Benjamin C. Taylor, pastor of the Bergen Dutch Reformed Church, characterized the fallen mayor as having been quick to forgive his attackers, remarking that "the assault made upon him, he attributed to no evil intent upon him personally but to the madness and ferocity of the hour, and he could individually forgive it all."

The mayor, who left behind a widow and six children, was laid to rest in the Speers Cemetery on Van Wagen Street in the town of Bergen. As the Civil War dragged on for four more years, it brought with it a deluge of casualties and the newspapers published long and doleful lists of local fallen heroes. Mayor Carpenter's story faded alongside such tragedies. No public markers, parks or buildings are dedicated to this public servant who gave his life in an effort to keep peace between his community and Union soldiers, nor is there any trace of Carpenter's grave, as the marker and exact resting place can no longer be found in the Speer Cemetery. He has, until now, been lost to time. (Winfield, *History of the County of Hudson*; Carpenter, *History and Genealogy of the Carpenter Family*; US Census, 1860; Todd, *American Military Equipage*; Jersey City *Courier*; New York *Tribune*; *Daily Gazette*; *New York Reformer*; *American Standard*; *New York Times*. Special thanks to Bob Murgittroyd for research assistance and guidance.)

New Jersey Civil War Myths
by
Jim Stephens

There are many misunderstandings about New Jersey's conduct during the Civil War. Of all the states that remained loyal to the Union, none was as suspect as New Jersey. The southern tier of the state was below the Mason-Dixon Line. It was the only Northern state that failed to give all its electoral votes to Abraham Lincoln in both 1860 and 1864. It sent a copperhead to the United States Senate. It was the only Union state that still had slaves. Surely it was a hotbed of Confederate sympathy. Nothing could be further from the truth.

Perhaps the most persistent myth is that South Jersey was supportive of the Confederate cause as it lay below the Mason-Dixon Line, the boundary between the free state of Pennsylvania and the slave states of Maryland and Delaware. If extended

A Mason-Dixon line marker along the Maryland/Pennsylvania border (Henry F. Ballone)

eastward, the east-west segment of this border, named after the men who surveyed it from 1763 to 1767, Charles Mason and Jeremiah Dixon, would reach the Atlantic in the vicinity of Harvey Cedars on Long Beach Island. The location of much of the southern portion of New Jersey below this line is, however, nothing more than an accident of geography. Rather than casting their lot with the South, during the election of 1860, the eight counties of South Jersey (Burlington, Ocean, Camden, Atlantic, Gloucester, Salem, Cumberland and Cape May) cast the majority of their presidential votes for Abraham Lincoln. Lincoln's support was strong in the region. In a unique display of enthusiasm for the candidate sometimes known as "The Railsplitter," on Election Day 1860, Atlantic County Republicans staged an elaborate march led by a man on a wagon splitting cedar logs into fence rails.

Far below the Mason-Dixon Line in New Jersey's southernmost county, Cape May, not only did Lincoln win, but Republicans swept every office on the ballot. The 1st Congressional District, encompassing much of southern New Jersey, was represented by a Republican, John Nixon. When war came in 1861, the people of South Jersey were quick to demonstrate against secession and rush to the colors in defense of the Union.

A footnote to the secessionist South Jersey myth is the prewar popularity of the community of Cape Island (as the city of Cape May was known prior to 1869) as a summer resort destination for southern planters. Though true, the seasonal presence of men who owned large numbers of slaves did nothing to steer the people of Cape May County toward support for disunion. Using a modern analogy, New Jersey historian William Gillette notes "many Canadians vacation on the Jersey Shore, yet no one assumes that this amounts to a vital Canadian connection that influences the political behavior of New Jerseyans." While the people of Cape Island certainly appreciated the income they earned from their Southern guests, this did not result in unity with the Southern cause.

Another piece of "evidence" contributing to the myth of New Jersey's supposed secessionist leanings is the fact that it was the only Union state that failed to give its electoral votes to Abraham Lincoln in both the elections of 1860 and 1864. Lincoln won four of Jersey's seven electoral votes in 1860, but did not receive any in 1864. This is frequently used to imply that New Jersey only reluctantly remained in the Union. There are actually simple reasons why the state voted as it did, none of them having to do with Confederate tendencies. First, New Jersey was, and still remains today, a Democratic-leaning state, so Jersey's support of Democratic candidates is part of a broad historical pattern. In 1860, Jersey's electoral votes were split between Lincoln and another candidate from Illinois, the nationally renowned and respected United States Senator Stephen A. Douglas, nominee of the Northern Democrats. The Southern Democrat candidate, Vice President John Breckinridge of Kentucky, found little support in New Jersey despite winning the electoral votes of neighboring Delaware. In 1860, it is important to remember that Lincoln was still an unknown quantity to many voters. But certainly by 1864 he was far from unknown. Why didn't New Jersey support him then? The answer lies with the second reason for New Jersey's Civil War presidential voting pattern, the Democratic candidate for the presidency in 1864. Following his dismissal from command of the Army of the Potomac in the fall of 1862, Major General George B. McClellan moved his family to Orange in New Jersey's Essex County. As a resident of New Jersey during his campaign as the Democratic Party's nominee for the presidency in 1864, this circumstance made McClellan a "favorite son" in the state, enabling him to win Jersey's electoral votes. As in 1860, the eight-county South Jersey region would once again cast the majority of its votes for Lincoln, but this would be of no help to the president due to a situation that is as true today as it was during the Civil War; the vast majority of the state's population lived in the northern half of the state, a region far more Democratic than sparsely populated, Republican-leaning South Jersey. Though McClellan lost the presidential race in 1864, he continued to be popular in New Jersey, serving as governor from 1878 to 1881.

The war began optimistically, but following the First Battle of Bull Run in July 1861, many in the North began to realize the conflict would not be ended by one or two grand engagements. Following battlefield setbacks in 1862, particularly the Army of the Potomac's bloody repulse at Fredericksburg, a faction of the Democratic Party argued that a negotiated end to the conflict was necessary, even if it resulted in recognition of Confederate independence. After September 1862, they were also vocal opponents of the Emancipation Proclamation. Known by their supporters as Peace Democrats and by their opponents as copperheads, their influence increased in 1863. Their most notable member at the national level was Ohio Congressman Clement Vallandigham.

As part of an internal political manuever, James W. Wall, a notorious "copperhead," was elected a US Senator by the NJ legislature in 1863 to serve out six weeks remaining in deceased Senator John R. Thomson's term. (Library of Congress)

Another part of the myth of Southern sympathy in New Jersey has to do with a copperhead who became one of the state's U. S. Senators. A lawyer and outspoken opponent of the war from the beginning, James Wall of Burlington was a strong believer in free speech and a free press, even during wartime. Wall felt President Lincoln's policies were usurping the Constitution. When the U. S. Post Office seized copies of a New Jersey newspaper that had been deemed seditious, Wall wrote a forceful letter to the postmaster general protesting his actions. His note brought a swift response; he was arrested and imprisoned in New York. He was released two weeks later only after swearing an oath of allegiance to the United States. Wall thus came to be considered a martyr by many Democrats.

When U. S. Senator John Renshaw Thomson died in September 1862, a replacement was needed to fill the remainder of his term, which would end in March 1863. In the era before the Seventeenth Amendment, senators were selected by state legislatures. However, as the legislature was out of session, outgoing Republican Governor Charles Olden made an appointment that would last until the legislators returned in January. The Republicans had lost control in the November 1862 legislative election, meaning that Democrats would get to make a choice to fill out the last few weeks of the U.S. Senate term before making a full-term selection in March. Governor Olden picked Richard Field. During the recent election, Field had proven to be an extreme partisan, routinely referring to nearly all Democrats as "traitors." In his few weeks in Washington, he continued his attacks. His support of the Lincoln administration won the notice of the president, who gave him a federal district court judgeship when he left the Senate on January 14, 1863.

The incoming Democratic legislators had two objectives in mind when they met in January 1863, revenge and tactical politics. Rather than having succumbed to secessionism, Democrats who supported the war effort believed that by giving the short term to a copperhead, that group might be willing to support a member of the war faction for the six-year term. After several votes, the Democratic caucus chose Wall. After suffering Field's abuse, sending the notorious Wall to replace him would be payback. Wall had to be persuaded to take the post and had actually traveled to Trenton to ask to be taken out of the contest. Nonetheless, he eventually accepted and made his way to Washington. Wall's brief time in the Senate was without incident but his presence there was an embarrassment to mainstream Democrats and to another important wartime constituency, New Jersey's soldiers. In the end, Wall's short stay in the Senate meant little. To see it today as a symptom of support for the Confederacy, rather than the tawdry political maneuver it actually was, is a gross misinterpretation.

The final piece of the myth of Civil War New Jersey concerns the institution of slavery. New Jersey is occasionally referred to as the only Union state that still had slaves. This overlooks the glaring fact that the slave states of Delaware, Maryland, Kentucky and Missouri had remained in the Union with varying degrees of enthusiasm.

Slavery had existed in colonial New Jersey, as it had in all 13 colonies. Early English land grants permitted slavery. The colony's proprietors offered incentives to settlers who imported slaves. In 1664, residents were granted an additional 60 acres of land for each slave they owned. Dr. Daniel Coxe, absentee governor of West Jersey from 1687 to 1692, is known to have imported slaves to work in some of the   concerns he established on his vast 95,000-acre landholdings that stretched from north of Trenton, south to the Cape May peninsula. Following the Revolution, slavery began to wane in the northern states, gradually being legislated away. In 1804, New Jersey became the last state in the northeast to take steps to end slavery. The state legislature planned to do so gradually. As of July 4, 1804, children of slave parents were to be granted their freedom after serving as "apprentices" to their mother's master. Males would be freed at age 25, females at the age of 21. Protests by abolitionist groups to Jersey's gradual approach led to modification of the law in 1846. Slavery was formally forbidden; those still held in bondage were not emancipated but officially reclassified as "apprentices for life." African-American children born to those still enslaved after the law's passage were declared free, though those still legally categorized as apprentices were obligated to remain in that status for life, but could not be sold without obtaining their permission.

Age steadily thinned the ranks of those trapped in the position of apprentice. Though New Jersey law used the term "apprentice," the census of 1860 counted them using the name for what they actually were: slave. The "New Jersey as slave state" myth implies that the numbers of apprentices/slaves was large. In fact, the final census tally showed that there were just 18 of them, all elderly people either employed as house servants or retired from work due to age and infirmity. New Jersey Civil War mythology also insinuates that slaves were likely to be found "below the Mason-Dixon Line" in South Jersey. However, the census showed that not a single "apprentice for life" lived anywhere in the eight southern counties of the state; all were located in northern New Jersey. They resided in Bergen, Somerset, Hunterdon, Passaic, Middlesex, Morris and Union counties. While the presence of slavery in New Jersey into the 1860s is not a fact in which we can take pride, their very small numbers were no more an influence on Jersey's allegiance than were the Southern planters that vacationed in Cape Island.

There is much about mid-nineteenth-century New Jersey that, 150 years later, is repulsive to us. Free African-Americans were viewed with suspicion. Some extreme copperheads agitated to have them forced from the state. Racism of the ugliest sort was common and President Lincoln's Emancipation Proclamation was unpopular with many state residents. Nonetheless, these facts did not reflect support for the Confederacy. To most New Jerseyans of the Civil War era, secession equaled treason and that alone was sufficient reason to support the war. To imply otherwise is to dishonor the memory of those of our ancestors who sacrificed so much for the cause of the Union. (Cunningham, *New Jersey: America's Main Road*; Gillette, *Jersey Blue*; Wright, *Afro-Americans in New Jersey*)

Trains, Ships and Guns –
New Jersey's Civil War Production Line
by
John Kuhl

Although New Jersey's industrial production has declined in recent years, at the end of World War II only six other states exceeded the Garden State in the value of their products. The state's manufacturing preeminence was longstanding. At the advent of the industrial age in the early 19th century, New Jersey's inherent advantages,

The Trenton Iron Works
(Woodward & Hageman, *History of Burlington and Mercer*)

including proximity to leading national urban markets and ports, abundant iron deposits, energy resources in the form of wood, coal and water, and an early infrastructure of railroads and canals, all combined to stimulate commercial growth.

Paterson, Alexander Hamilton's choice for an industrial city and the location of Samuel Colt's first revolver factory in the 1830s, and Newark, where inventive genius Seth Boyden created patent leather, as well as Trenton, Camden and a number of smaller New Jersey cities, developed into important manufacturing centers by the mid-19th century. Although rocked by the Panic of 1857, which led to a significant loss of business and an abrupt population decline in Newark, at the time of the Civil War the state was still a major manufacturing center for leather goods, ships, iron, paper products, textiles, pottery and glassware.

In 1861, New Jersey copperhead politicians predicted economic disaster in the wake of secession, war and the consequent loss of Southern markets for leather and luxury goods, as well as for cheap slave clothing produced in the state. But after an initial recession, the Civil War led to an industrial boom as New Jersey strove to meet the needs of the armed forces. Paterson's silk weavers quickly transitioned to making woolen army uniforms. Halsey, Hunter and Company, a leading Newark clothier, made enormous profits supplying its wares to the Union army, as did, ironically, a company belonging to copperhead congressman Nehemiah Perry. Newark's leather producers became major suppliers of shoes, harness, belts, cartridge boxes and other military necessities to both state and national governments. The New Jersey quartermaster-general's reports for the war years reveal a vast variety of purchases of New Jersey-manufactured goods for the state's soldiers, including leather equipment, uniforms, hats, overcoats, socks, blankets, and underwear.

In the antebellum years, the state's ship builders, located on both the Hudson and Delaware rivers, produced wooden ships for naval and civilian service, with nearby Hunterdon County forests providing some of the heavy oak timber for their construction. When the navy turned increasingly to steam-powered ironclad ships during the war, New Jersey shipyards quickly adapted to accommodate demand, so expanding a major industry that it thrived well into the 20th century until a post-World War II decline.

The versatile Stevens family of Hoboken, pioneers in New Jersey railroading, were also early naval innovators. Before the war, Edwin and Robert Stevens worked on a government contract to develop a floating "iron steam battery," which was actually an ironclad ship. Although the "battery" was never accepted by the navy, and eventually scrapped in 1874, the design skills the brothers honed while working on it were easily transferred to the construction of double-ended gunboats like the USS *Mohongo* and ironclad *Passaic*-class "monitors," including the USS *Weehawken*, in Jersey City. Perhaps the most famous Jersey City-built monitor was the USS *Tecumseh*. Jerseyman chief engineer John Faron supervised the ship's construction, and then sailed on it under Lieutenant Commander T. A. M. Craven of Bound Brook. While leading the attack on Mobile Bay in 1864, *Tecumseh* struck a mine, rolled over and sank in twenty-five seconds with the loss of Craven, Faron, and 90 others from its crew of about 100 men.

The Civil War marked the first major use of railroads to move troops and supplies in war. The first railway in the United States, the Camden and Amboy, facilitated by Edwin A. Stevens' introduction of the T-rail to America, began operations in New Jersey in 1832. It is unsurprising, then, that New Jersey became a hub of railroad development and manufacturing prior to the outbreak of hostilities in 1861.

Greatly increased wartime demand for raw material to make engines, cars and tracks proved a bonanza for many small iron-making firms throughout the state, including the Taylor Works in High Bridge. Lambertville, Trenton, and Jersey City factories produced railroad engines prior to or during the war, but Paterson, home to locomotive makers Rogers, Danforth-Cooke and Swinburne-Smith, was a national leader in steam-engine manufacture prior to, during and after the conflict. Two Paterson-built locomotives made history in 1862 when Union raiders hijacked the Western & Atlantic Railroad of Georgia's *General*, built in 1855 by Rogers, and were chased down by three other locomotives, including the *Texas*, an 1856 product of Danforth-Cooke. Both engines survived the war and are on museum display today.

The short-lived prewar Trenton Locomotive Works played a wartime role in a different field, small-arms manufacturing. The firm of Burt and Hodge leased the Locomotive Works' vacated factory, a few blocks northeast of

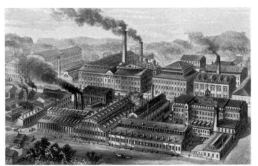

A postwar view of the Rogers locomotive factory in Paterson, where the *General* was built in 1855. (*Locomotives & Locomotive Building*)

today's Trenton Thunder baseball stadium, to manufacture U. S. Model 1861 pattern .58 caliber rifle-muskets. Burt and Hodge made some parts and purchased others, including rifled barrels made by the Trenton Iron Company, located nearby along the Delaware River. By the time Burt and Hodge ceased production in 1864, it had supplied 22,995 rifle-muskets to the federal government, 5,300 to the state of New Jersey and an unknown number to other states. The state-purchased rifle-muskets, surcharged "NJ," were issued to militia units and

The *General*, a Paterson-built engine that played a major role in the legendary "great locomotive chase." (Marty Boa)

then stored at the state arsenal through the turn of the 20th century, when they were sold to surplus dealers, including Bannerman's of New York City.

The Trenton Locomotive Works factory was also the site of the Wiard Ordnance Works, which manufactured a variety of cannons, from light field pieces to heavy siege guns, including H.F. Mann's 20,000-pound, eight-inch breech-loading rifle, the first of its kind. The state arsenal, located next to the state prison in Trenton, was a busy place during the war as well, with state employees converting flintlock muskets to percussion-ignition, storing and issuing large supplies of weapons and other equipment, as well as cleaning, repairing and reissuing small arms.

Newark also had its small-arms makers, including Hewes and Phillips, a company that supplemented state in-house efforts to convert flintlock muskets to percussion early in the war. "H&P" converted 8,000 muskets for the state and another 12,000 for the federal government. The Manhattan Firearms Company was founded in 1856 by a group of New Jersey businessmen who established a factory in Newark in 1859, which produced over 125,000 handguns through 1873, most of them .36 caliber arms resembling the famed Colt Navy revolver. A few Manhattans were acquired by the government but most were privately purchased by individual officers as personal side arms.

Both Trenton and Newark boasted well-known edged-weapon manufacturers. Newark cutler Henry Sauerbier, who opened a business in the city in 1848, became a well-known maker of high-grade swords for army officers, both for field use and as presentation pieces, during the war. Most of Sauerbier's sales were to individuals, with his government work limited to a contract for 100 foot-officer swords.

The leading New Jersey sword maker was, without doubt, James Emerson of the Trenton firm of Emerson and Silver. Using the engraving skills of an inmate of the nearby state prison, Emerson turned out very high-grade presentation swords, such as the one for Commodore Charles Boggs of New Brunswick, the "Hero of New Orleans" in 1862. Emerson received large federal and state contracts for enlisted men's swords, as well. He later claimed that he had made 100,000 swords for the government but available federal contract totals only substantiate deliveries of 27,000 light cavalry sabers, 12,000 noncommissioned-officer swords, 3,000 musician swords and 10,000 "camp hatchets." The total of Emerson and Silver's sales to various states during the war is currently unknown, but the company supplied the state of New Jersey with 1,000 cavalry sabers, 300 artillery sabers and 200 noncommissioned-officer swords in 1863. Emerson provided more durable metal rather than leather scabbards with his swords, which led to a government contract with the company for experimental metal bayonet scabbards with an innovative swivel.

Anti-war Newark Congressman Nehemiah Perry made a large amount of money selling uniforms to the Union army. (National Archives)

By the end of the Civil War, New Jersey's citizens had every reason to be as proud of the state's efficient and diverse manufacturing base as they were of the military accomplishments of its soldiers, sailors, and marines on the battlefield. New Jersey-made clothing and weapons were not only present on many a battlefield, but ships and trains built in the state were responsible for getting the forces of the Union where they had to be in order to win the war. (*NJQMG Reports, 1860-1905*; Bazelon & MGuinn, *Directory*; Flayderman, *Guide*; Sutherland & Wilson, *Colt Firearms*; Tuttle, *How Newark Became Newark*; Myers, *Story of New Jersey*; Aiken, *Great Locomotive Chase*; Kennedy, ed. *New Jersey Almanac*; *Hunterdon County Democrat*; *Hunterdon Republican*; *Lambertville Beacon*; *Hunterdon Gazette*)

Albert Beach and the Manhattan Revolver
by
Thomas R. Burke

Albert Beach was born in Newark, New Jersey, in 1819. In 1855, Beach, a successful Newark businessman, became a major investor in and secretary of the newly formed Manhattan Fire Arms Company, incorporated in New York City. Since Beach and his associates had no actual knowledge of firearms design or manufacturing, they hired the experienced Thomas Bacon as factory superintendent. Although the principals of Manhattan Firearms were from Newark, initial production began in neither New York nor New Jersey, but in Norwich, Connecticut, that state then being the heart of the American firearms industry. The company made a variety of inexpensive single-shot pistols and revolving-barrel handguns of "pepperbox" configuration.

In 1859, the Manhattan factory moved to Newark, relocating to a building at the corner of Orange and High streets. Since Samuel Colt's patents had expired in 1857, Manhattan began making clones of the Colt .31 caliber Pocket and .36 caliber Navy revolvers at the Newark address. The main difference between the Colt and the

A Newark-made Manhattan revolver (Jerry Backoff)

Manhattan was that the latter had extra hammer-rest safety notches between the chambers. In addition to these percussion-ignition guns, Manhattan made .22 caliber rim-fire cartridge revolvers. During the company's existence, Manhattan Firearms became a major handgun manufacturer, producing approximately 150,000 handguns, more than any other maker during those years save Colt and Remington.

Newark address was stamped on Manhattan revolver barrels. (Jerry Backoff)

Beach and his associates, in common with other manufacturers, knew that the figurative pot of gold of the firearms business was large military contracts, and no doubt saw the outbreak of the Civil War as a golden opportunity. Although federal contracts never materialized, save for possibly one small order, Manhattan sold a considerable number of revolvers to individual officers and soldiers.

Albert Beach, his wife Maria and their five children lived on the "Old Bloomfield Road" in the Newark suburb of Woodside, today's Belleville, New Jersey, where he helped found Christ Church in 1871. In 1865, Beach, a highly regarded member of the Newark business community, was a member of the committee that organized President Lincoln's funeral procession through the city in a ceremony that included a lengthy parade, fireworks and a speech by Frederick T. Frelinghuysen.

In 1868, wartime demands behind it, Manhattan Fire Arms changed its name to the American Standard Tool Company and expanded its production to include industrial tools and hardware as well as a limited number of firearms. The company went out of business during the financial panic of 1873. Albert Beach died in the early 1880s, although the exact date of his passing is unknown. (Flayderman, *Flayderman's Guide*; McCaulay, *Civil War Pistols;* bit.ly/Newarkfirearm; Nutter, *Manhattan Firearms)*

Cape May at War
by
Jim Stephens

New Jersey's south-ernmost county presented a far different face to the world in 1861 than it does in the 21st century. While a summer tourism economy existed in Cape Island (as the city of Cape May was known prior to 1869), the rest of the county was still primarily rural and agricul-tural, "clusters of houses rather than a community of towns" according to histo-rian Jeffery Dorwart. Farm-land was abundant along the roads that connected the county's small villages. Along waterways in Goshen, Dennisville, Beesley's Point, Marshallville and Tuckahoe, shipyards produced oceangoing sailing vessels. Mar-shallville also featured a prosperous glassworks that turned out bottles and window glass. Fishermen harvested a wealth of oysters and fish from the Atlantic Ocean and Delaware Bay. The county's plentiful supply of cedar fueled a busy shingle-making industry. The barrier islands along the county's eastern shoreline were only acces-sible by boat, virtually uninhabited and covered by forests of cedar and holly. Though by 1860 Cape May County's population had grown to 7,136, many of those citizens could trace their ancestry back to the families that had migrated from New England and eastern Long Island to settle the peninsula in the late 17th century.

The United States Hotel in Cape Island, where Company A, 7th New Jersey Volunteer Infantry was organized in the summer of 1861. (Cape May County Museum)

South Jersey is unjustly said to have been a region sympathetic to the Confederate cause, but facts do not support that view. In the election of 1860, Cape May County voters cast the majority of their ballots for Abraham Lincoln, 680 to 520, and the county sent Republican John Nixon to Congress. Additionally, all county offices up for election in 1860 were won by Republicans. Though the Democratic presidential candidate in 1864 was quasi-favorite son George McClellan, who had moved to New Jersey following his dismissal from command of the Army of the Potomac, Cape May County supported President Lincoln by 761 to 557. Following Lincoln's assassination, mass meetings were held in Cape Island and Cape May Court House to mourn his passing.

Despite Cape May County's southerly location, the area showed little enthusiasm for the Confederate cause. In a rare act of support for disunion, a South Carolina palmetto flag was hoisted to the top of a flagpole in Cape Island in February 1861. It was promptly taken down and burned. The bombardment of

Cape May Court House as it appeared at the time of the Civil War. (Cape May County Museum)

Fort Sumter on April 12, 1861, generated support for the cause of the Union. "The fiendish Davis & Co. fired the first shots," wrote a correspondent to the Cape Island *Ocean Wave* newspaper, "and no one can tell who will fire the last." At an "enthusiastic war meeting" on April 27 in the county seat of Cape May Court House, participants resolved "to stand by our state and national governments, to maintain the Union, the Constitution and the laws and protect our national flag from further insult." A mass meeting in Rio Grande burned Confederate leader Jefferson Davis in effigy. Citizens of Goshen expressed their support for the Union in a simpler fashion. A flag was attached to the top of a "cedar pole 60 feet in height." The assembled group then gave "three hearty cheers for the Union, three cheers for the president and three groans for Southern and Northern traitors."

Relative proximity to the new Confederacy caused concern among some. A Lower Township man, concerned that Confederate President Davis was recruiting privateers to raid Union shipping and coastlines, invoked memories of British raids on the peninsula during the War of 1812: "There is no question but before two weeks our waters will be blackened with these piratical craft…and one of the places of rendezvous will be Delaware Bay. It is altogether likely that they will at times effect a landing on our coast and…pursue their thieving in our midst." In response, a militia company was formed "to greet [privateers] with a salute of hot lead." The home guard's service would, however, be uneventful; the privateers never arrived.

Like others across the United States, men of Cape May County offered their services to suppress the rebellion. In July 1861, a meeting at the United States Hotel in Cape Island resulted in the formation of the Cape May Guards. The Guards left for Trenton in September, where they would lose their dashing designation when they were mustered into the army as Company A of the 7th New Jersey Volunteers. Cape May County men could also be found in the 9th, 12th , 25th and 38th regiments, the 1st New Jersey Cavalry and various regiments of the United States Colored Troops. Mounting casualties would complicate recruiting. By 1863, the county was budgeting large sums to provide bounties to entice men to enlist. Towns competed to fill their quotas to avoid a draft. In 1864, a group of men had each been promised $700 for enlisting from Middle Township. After arriving in Trenton, they changed their place of enlistment to New Brunswick when an agent from that community approached them with an offer of $800. By 1865, 32 Cape May County soldiers had given their lives.

Two of the county's volunteers stood out from the rest. Cape Island carpenter Henry Sawyer, after visiting Governor Charles Olden to seek a military appointment and traveling to Washington for the governor, found himself a lieutenant in the newly formed 1st New Jersey Cavalry. By 1863, Sawyer had risen to the rank of captain. At Brandy Station, Virginia, he was severely wounded. Taken to Richmond's infamous Libby Prison, he was at the center of an incident that gained national attention.

As reprisal for two Confederate captains who had been executed as spies, Jefferson Davis ordered the captains at Libby to draw lots, with two men selected to be put to death. Sawyer and Captain John Flynn were the unfortunate pair. Sawyer's wife contacted Congressman John Nixon and met with President Lincoln. Lincoln's threat to execute Robert E. Lee's son "Rooney" Lee if Sawyer and Flynn were harmed caused Davis to rescind his order. Sawyer was exchanged in early 1864 and returned to service. Following the war, Sawyer opened the Chalfonte Hotel and greeted many notable visitors to Cape May before his death in 1893.

Another distinguished Cape May County fighting man was Goshen native Andrew Tomlin. Serving with the United States Marine Corps, Tomlin was a corporal in the Marine contingent aboard the frigate USS *Wabash*. In January 1865, the *Wabash* participated in the second attempt to take Fort Fisher, North Carolina. Tomlin was among those sent ashore to take part in the assault. Charged with holding a trench line at the rear of the fort, Tomlin and 200 Marines held off several Confederate attacks. When a comrade was wounded, Tomlin risked his life to rescue the injured man. For his valor, Tomlin earned the Medal of Honor. He became sheriff of Cape May County in 1895.

Those at home would also aid the war effort. By 1863, women had formed soldiers' aid societies in every community in the county. They worked to provide for the needs of local men who had gone to war, as well as to support army hospitals. Typical of these groups was the Middle Township Soldiers' Aid Society, which reported that during February 1864 they had "forwarded the following hospital supplies: 17 red flannel shirts, 17 pairs of flannel drawers, 52 pairs of wool socks, 13 large feather pillows," as well as a wide variety of other useful items.

Kennedy's pharmacy in Cape May proudly flew a US flag during the war. (Cape May County Museum)

The most important event to occur in the county during the war had nothing to do with the conflict. Travel to the county by land was difficult. In the early 19th century, a stagecoach journey from Camden to Cape Island was an arduous trip of two days. By 1861, a railroad had been completed from Camden to Millville, but for Cape May County residents the trip to Camden still took nearly a day. That would change in 1863 with the construction of the Cape May and Millville Railroad. Despite a shortage of laborers, two teams began construction in March. One group worked south from Millville, the other laying track northward from Cape Island. By June, the people of Cape Island heard the whistle of a locomotive for the first time as operations began along the section of line that had reached Cape May Court House. By August the two teams met.

As local resident Amelia Hand noted, "We at last have a Rail Road from Cape Island to Philadelphia and August 26 the cars made the trip for the first time, the route was performed in three and a half hours, quite an improvement over our old way of going to Philadelphia." The railroad would stimulate Cape Island's summer tourism, which had declined since 1861. By war's end, new hotels were being constructed. The railroad would begin serving the barrier islands in 1879, spurring development of those previously barren places.

Relative to the rest of New Jersey, Cape May County may have been deep in the south but the people of the Jersey Cape never wavered in their support of the cause of the North. (Bilby and Goble, *Jerseymen*; Cunningham, *Railroads in New Jersey*; Dorwart, *Cape May County*; Gillette, *Jersey Blue*; *Ocean Wave*; Cold Spring Village Interpretive Manuals)

New Jersey's Jewish Community and the Civil War
by
Bruce M. Form

The migration of people of the Jewish faith to what became the United States began in 1654, when a ship containing some twenty-four unwanted Jewish refugees landed in the Dutch colony of New Amsterdam at the direction of the Dutch West India Company over the protest of Governor Peter Stuyvesant. From these ambivalent beginnings, Jews have always been a representative segment of the American population.

In the initial decades of the 19th century, the Jewish population of America did not increase at a rapid rate. At the time of the first United States census in 1790, it was estimated that there were at most two-thousand Jews in a national population of four-million people, and by the year 1850, after the United States had experienced an expansion of territorial growth and a population rise to twenty-three million, there were still only about five-thousand Jews in the country. Although there were Jews living in New Jersey from its earliest days, even when it was part of New Netherland, Jewish social and religious life in the state had not evolved into a centralized synagogue-based community by 1850. The major Jewish population and cultural centers in the United States at the time were located in large cities like New York, Philadelphia, Cincinnati, Baltimore and Louisville.

In the decade leading up to the Civil War, however, the American Jewish population expanded dramatically as part of the massive influx into the country of immigrants from Ireland, England, Germany and central Europe. By 1860 there were approximately 150,000 Jewish men, women and children in the United States. The decade also witnessed major increases in the Jewish population of the New Jersey cities of Newark, New Brunswick and Trenton, and the appearance of synagogues led to a more identifiably structured Jewish community. At the outbreak of the Civil War, New Jersey's Jews proved as patriotic and motivated as their Christian fellow citizens in doing their part to preserve the Union. That patriotism was expressed in many forms, including going to the front as soldiers, assisting with the care of the sick and wounded, and supporting the Union war effort at home through business or community service.

As in all American conflicts prior to and after the Civil War, New Jersey's Jews served with distinction in the United States military. Research has documented a minimum of 277 Jewish Jerseymen serving in the state's units, including in twenty-nine of its infantry regiments, all three New Jersey cavalry regiments and Batteries A and C of the New Jersey light artillery. According to historian Simon Wolf, another 161 Jewish New Jerseyans served in the volunteer regiments of other states or as sailors on various vessels in the Union navy. It is difficult to determine how many Jewish sailors from New Jersey served during the Civil War because naval personnel records are based upon each ship's complement of officers and men, not their states of origin. It should be noted, however, that at the outbreak of the war the highest-ranking officer in the United States Navy, although he was not from New Jersey, was a Jewish officer, Commodore Uriah P. Levy.

The Jewish soldier served with the same pride and suffered through the same horrors as his non-Jewish comrades in arms or "pards" during the Civil War. One of those soldiers was Hardy Deetlebach, a young boy who ran away from his home in New Jersey in 1864 and lied about his age to enlist in another state under the name Charles Watten so that his mother would not know he had joined the army. Once Deetlebach, claiming he was 18-years old, mustered into service in Company K of the 9th New Hampshire Volunteers and was in the front lines in Virginia, he contacted his mother by letter to let her know where he was, and continued a correspondence with her while she, in turn, petitioned both New Jersey governor Joel Parker and President Abraham Lincoln in an attempt to get him discharged as underage.

Young Deetlebach's letters home told of everyday events and his military experiences: From Bristoe Station on May 2, "… Mosbey's Gorillas [sic] are on all sides of us and we have pickets out in the woods all the time." Spotsylvania Court House, May 14, "…Our regiment has been fighting now for 11 days and have not got through yet. Out of 55 men that belonged to my Company there are 20 left, the rest are either killed, wounded or missing…" At "1 mile from Petersburg, July 23, 1864," Deetlebach wrote, " … Lt. Allen is back in the rear with the cooks at present, he is sick…. I saw an American eagle this morning he measured about 7-1/2 feet from tip to tip. He belonged to the 37th Wisconsin Regiment. They brought him along from Wisconsin…The report here is that the Paymaster from the 9th Army Corps will be here next week to pay off the soldiers. If we get paid I shall send the largest part of my money home…" Near Poplar Grove Church, Virginia, October 24, 1864, he advised, "…I had a fit a few mornings ago and one of the men went down and told the Doctor, and what do you think the brute told the man? He said to let him 'fit', I can't do anything for him and neither can my medicine… There is also a good deal of excitement here about the [presidential] election. I also think that Lincoln will get it, but I hope that 'Little Mac' will beat him." In his last letter home in November 1864, Hardy wrote from "near Pegram House, Virginia," that "…I have not been examined yet by any surgeon but I will let you know as soon as I am examined. There is [was] an election in this regiment today for President but the most of them voted for Lincoln. They only let legalized voters vote….I would like to have one more shirt and my boots for the rainy weather is coming now." Private Hardy Deetlebach, a.k.a. Charles Watten, died of pneumonia in camp before word of his discharge reached him.

Another New Jersey Jewish infantryman was German-born Sigmund Eckstein, who volunteered on August 5, 1864, at age thirty-two, to serve as a substitute for draftee William Dougal for a period of three-years service. Eckstein was assigned to Company E of the 8th New Jersey Volunteer Infantry and was wounded by a gunshot to the right leg with a laceration of the tibial artery at Petersburg on November 16. Carried from the field to the City Point hospital, he died of his wound there the same day.

Charles Friedlander enlisted in the Union army on August 13, 1863, in Jersey City and then was sent to Camp Parker in Trenton for assignment to the newly formed 2nd New Jersey Volunteer Cavalry, where he became a private in Company

B. Under the command of Colonel Joseph Karge, the 2nd traveled first to Virginia, and then to the western theater of war. On June 10, 1864, at the battle of Brice's Crossroads, Mississippi, Friedlander was reported missing in action and presumed captured. William Goldsmith, a carpenter from Bloomfield Township, enlisted in the 2nd New Jersey Infantry's Company G on May 28, 1861. Private Goldsmith fought in all of his regiment's battles through May 14, 1864, when he was captured by the enemy at Spotsylvania Court House. Both of these Jewish Jerseymen ended up in the infamous Andersonville Prison in Georgia. Like so many other prisoners at Andersonville, Friedlander and Goldsmith both died of disease there, and are buried in the Andersonville National Cemetery.

The Jewish Community of New Jersey not only contributed military personnel to the struggle to save the Union. German Jewish immigrants Henry Sire and his wife, Rosena, settled in Morristown, where they farmed and raised horses before the Civil War. Sire developed a large stable and became a respected horse dealer. His farm provided a number of remounts to the Union cavalry.

Just as their non-Jewish neighbors, Jewish civilians in New Jersey did whatever they could to help the war effort. Through their synagogues or independently, women joined aid societies to assist sick and wounded soldiers and became members of local sewing circles to provide extra clothing for soldiers. They also assumed responsibilities that had previously been reserved for men, becoming shopkeepers and business owners and running their farms when their men were away at the war. New Jersey's Jewish community was an active and integral part of the state's Civil War effort. (Korn, *American Jewry in the Civil War*; Tarshish, *Rise of American Judaism*; Wolf, *American Jew as Patriot*; Scherzer, *Early Jewish History in Morristown*; Deetlebach Letters, Metro West; NARA service and pension records)

Andersonville graves of Jewish New Jerseyans Charles Friedlander and William Goldsmith (Bruce & Mira Form)

Batter Up: New Jersey Base Ball and the Civil War
by
John Zinn

Baseball in New Jersey dates back to at least 1846, when Hoboken's Elysian Fields was the site of the New York Knickerbockers' historic match against the New York Base Ball Club. Active participation by New Jerseyans began during the late 1850's, when an estimated 130 clubs were formed, two-thirds of which were located in Newark and Jersey City. Although frequently thought of as a rural sport, baseball had its origins in urban areas where there were sufficient numbers of upper and middle-class young men in white-collar jobs with adequate leisure time. Some players were members of old New Jersey families, such as Edward Pennington and Stephen Plum of the Eureka Club of Newark, both of whom were descended from the city's founding families. While today's fans would recognize some aspects of the game, Civil War-era base ball (two words at the time) differed from modern baseball in important ways, including underhanded pitching, the absence of gloves and rules long since abandoned, such as batted balls caught on a bounce counting as outs.

That the Civil War would significantly impact baseball in New Jersey became obvious only a few short weeks after the surrender of Fort Sumter when the Newark Club (the state's first baseball team) was accused of refusing to allow its grounds to be used for military drill. Club president Henry Dusenberry indignantly denied the allegation, proclaiming proudly that the club had played under the national flag since 1855 "and now in this hour of our country's peril, we will be the last to withdraw from it our maintenance." The Newark Club's "maintenance" included at least eight members who backed up those words by service in the Union army. Two club members, James Conklin and Horace Smith, made the ultimate sacrifice at Gaines Mill in June of 1862.

In spite of reduced numbers, the Newark Club continued to play throughout the war, although with an abbreviated schedule. Their intra-city rival, the Eureka (arguably the best New Jersey club of the period), followed suit since a number of its members also were in the military. Especially noteworthy was R. Heber Breintnall, who served with the state militia and the 39th New Jersey, laying the groundwork for a long postwar career in the New Jersey National Guard, ultimately becoming the state's adjutant general.

Other New Jersey clubs responded differently to the conflict. The Liberty Club of New Brunswick, for example, suspended play for the duration of the war, even though few of its members appear to have served in the military. One who did serve was star shortstop Jarvis Wanser, who was an officer in the 14th New Jersey. After the war, Wanser served on the commission that erected the monument at the Monocacy battlefield and became the commandant of a home for veterans and their wives in Vineland. In their only 1861 match, the Liberty thrashed the Brooklyn Atlantic, the premier team of the era. It would be New Jersey's last victory over a New York team – and the Atlantic's last loss to a non-New York team — until after the war, when another New Jersey team would figure in an even bigger upset.

Although the Liberty resumed play in 1866, they never regained their pre-war form. The war may well have had an effect on the team's success much as World War II impacted the careers of many twentieth-century players, such as Hall of Famer Ted Williams.

With fewer regular matches to report on during the conflict, the *Newark Daily Advertiser* took notice of the state's earliest documented African-American team, the Hamilton Club of Newark. The black Newark men played and lost a September 1862 match to another African-American club from Long Island. Echoing the experience of matches between white clubs, the crowd included "a goodly number of the 'gentler sex.'"

Union soldiers playing base ball as POWs at Salisbury, North Carolina. (Currier & Ives)

Further anticipating the experience of twentieth-century wars, New Jersey baseball players who did not serve in the military supported the Union cause in other ways. In May of 1864, a select or "all star" team of New Jersey players traveled to Philadelphia to take on a similar team from the City of Brotherly Love in what was supposed to be a series of benefit games for the United States Sanitary Commission. Bad weather wiped out all but one game when some 2,000 people braved threatening weather to pay a 25-cents admission charge to witness the event. Not surprisingly, the New Jersey team featured four players from Newark, but also included young men from Princeton, Camden and Bridgeton. One of the Camden players, Weston Fishler, would later play in the first National League game in 1876. The game itself was a back-and-forth affair, with New Jersey clinging to a one-run lead before exploding for nine runs in the top of the sixth and coasting to an 18-10 victory. Readers of the next day's *Newark Daily Advertiser* could be excused for quickly skimming the paper's brief account of the game because of more pressing news – the first list of Newark residents drafted for military service. The paper saw humor in the fact that some of the names drawn from the wooden box (now in the collections of the New Jersey Historical Society) were either deceased or had been in the army since the war began.

With so many baseball players filling the ranks of New Jersey regiments, it is no surprise that baseball became a popular off-duty diversion for the Jersey boys, many of whom were away from home for the first time. Surviving records show that at least the 1st, 2nd, 5th, 8th, 11th, 21st and 26th regiments took part in baseball games either with other regiments or among themselves. After seeing a match between two New York regiments in the fall of 1861, the 1st and 2nd New Jersey regiments decided to follow suit. The initial match was delayed twice, once by weather and once by a review, before the 2nd defeated the 1st by 27-10. The umpire for this and a subsequent contest was James Conklin of the Newark Club, most likely the last baseball games he participated in before being killed at Gaines Mill. In reporting to the folks back home, a member of the 2nd New Jersey recognized the symbolic significance of such contests, noting, "We soon hope to have a good round game with the rebels and when we do, rest assured we will not get beaten but bring away the plume of victory." In April 1863, two teams from the 21st New Jersey played each other, which served as a warm-up for a contest with a New York unit the following month, which the Jerseymen won by a score of 26 to 25.

All of those matches occurred prior to Gettysburg, suggesting that the pace and spread of the war made continued play too difficult during the last years of the conflict. There would be one more, though - a swan song for New Jersey baseball in the army. On May 2, 1864, the 2nd New Jersey Infantry's team played the Harris Light (2nd New York) Cavalry. The score has gone unrecorded. It was the last game of a very short season.

Fortuitously for the 1865 season, the war's end in April allowed at least some New Jersey clubs to resume full activity. The Eureka Club of Newark had its best season that year in spite of two bitter one-run losses to the Brooklyn Atlantics, still the country's dominant team. By 1866, baseball was expanding rapidly throughout the state so that even small villages like Verona in Essex County had their own clubs. The 1866 season also saw what was arguably the biggest upset of the amateur era when an unknown club from the small farming village of Irvington lured the mighty Atlantics to their remote locale under the false pretenses of being a "poor country club." The Irvington Club, which included two future members of the Cincinnati Red Stockings (the nation's first all-professional team), handed the Brooklynites their first loss since 1863, ending their 43-game winning streak. The upset was symbolic that in baseball, as in many other aspects of American life, the Civil War marked a historical turning point. Things would never be the same again. (*Newark Daily Advertiser; New York Clipper*)

Modern day reenactors recreate 19th-century style base ball. (Mark Granieri)

"I Expect That the Horses and Wagons Have Gone to the Bottom"
Mud and the New Jersey Soldier, 1861-1865
by
Robert L. Silverman

It may seem hard to imagine today, but mid-19th-century American towns and cities were connected by dirt roads that were turned into seas of mud by rain or melting snow. Mud, the nemesis of soldiers throughout history, seems to have been commented on by Civil War soldiers more than most other unpleasant non-combat aspects of war. Although the armies usually went into winter quarters during the worst mud seasons of the year, rare was the soldier who did not have to slog through it and complain about it at one time or another. New Jersey soldiers were no exception, and what follows are excerpts from their letters, recounting for us their experiences in the muck, in their own unique words, spelling, and grammar:

"Since the morning following the night alarm described in my last letter the sky has been gloomy, and at intervals dropping its burdens either in dreary drizzles or saturating floods. This 'term' culminated yesterday afternoon in a tremendous thunder storm. Some tents were overthrown by the wind, and nearly all deluged. The camp of the 1st Regiment, which is located on lower ground than the others, was converted into a marsh. The boys took all the fun they could under the circumstances, and many of them could be seen sitting patiently under the pelting storm, with their fish lines thrown out into the puddles." — C. W. T. to the *Newark Daily Advertiser*, from Camp Princeton (Arlington, VA), 6/9/61

"We went abord of a steamer at the foot of E St. She brought us thirtyfive milds down the river and landed us in the damdest hole in America then we had ten milds to march about every half mild we had to waid a brook and when we wasent going through water we was in mud knee deep. I saw several wagon covers along the roaid in mud holes I expect the wagons and horses have gone to the bottom." — Private Isaac W. Rounsaville, Co. H, 6th NJVI, to William E. Haver, from Washington, DC, 12/5/61 (William E. Haver Papers, Hunterdon County Historical Society)

"On our return in passing through the City of Washington there was a great many remarks made about our appearances. Some of the boys were marching in their stocking feet their shoes being completely worn out as the roads was a complete map of mud." — Lieutenant William James Evans, 7th NJVI, to a friend, 12/?/61 (William J. Evans letters, New Jersey Historical Society)

"For a month past we have had some most fearful weather here. Rain! rain! Fog! fog! Mud! mud! Yes; mud! mud! mud! Quagmires! Mortar beds! Roads with the bottom fallen out!...My longlegged grey, 'Uncle Abe,' carried me through safely; but once or twice I really thought we would go through to China." — Lieutenant James F. Rusling, 5th NJVI, to friends, from camp on Lower Potomac, MD, 2/9/1862 (Rusling, *Men and Things I Saw*)

"Thanks to hard work and plenty of it, our corduroy road [built of logs] is done, and already named the 'Jersey Turnpike!' It is a splendid road, leading from our camp to Rum Point…'Abe,' who hates the mud awfully, neighs his satisfaction as soon as he reaches the turnpike, and canters cheerily along from end to end of it." — Lieutenant James F. Rusling, 5th NJVI, to his brother, from Lower Potomac, MD, 2/16/62 (Rusling, *Men and Things I Saw*)

"The roads were miserable, mud in many instances covering the boot entirely. Streams had to be forded and of course we were mud from head to foot….The best camping ground that could be found was a field quite muddy…At daybreak we resumed the march …we had to march in some instances through mud knee deep, and ford streams. All along the march when we felt thirsty our thirst was quenched by drinking out of some muddy pool, good water being scarce." — "Ego Ipse," Co. E, 12th NJVI, to the Woodbury *Constitution*, from camp near Endicott Mills, MD, 11/24/62

Lieutenant James F. Rusling, 5th NJ Volunteer Infantry (John Kuhl)

Captain Dayton Flint, 15th NJ Volunteer Infantry (John Kuhl)

"We have built up a little log house with a fireplace in it, and pitched our tent over it for a roof…The cracks between the logs we filled up with Virginia mud, which is a very peculiar kind of mud, and just now there is plenty of it. It sticks like molasses candy, and answers the place of mortar very well, besides being already mixed." — Corporal Dayton E. Flint, 15th NJVI, to his sister, from camp near White Oak Church, VA, 12/28/62 (Dayton Flint Letters, John Kuhl Collection)

"…Co. A was detailed to pull a load of pontoon lumber about a mile and a half…The boys took hold of the rope attached to the wagon, and, with deafening yells, extricated it from the mud and took it to its destination, and have thereby, earned the complimentary title of being 'Uncle Sam's mules.'…we moved toward White Oak Church over the muddiest road it has ever been my lot to witness; in some places it seemed impossible for us to wade through it. … It appears that the 'Rebs' were aware of our dilemma, as a large board was to be seen on the opposite shore, marked in large letters of chalk, 'Burnside Stuck In The Mud!' which has now become a by-word in the Army." — Sergeant Lucien A. Voorhees, Co. A, 15th NJVI, to the *Hunterdon Republican*, 1/27/63

"The weather has been so cold and stormy…it would rain one day and snow the next and then mud knee deep for that's the style of old Virginia… it rained for two days so the Army could not move. The Artilery and Pontoon train were hub deep in the mud and could not move until the mud dried a little. They put twenty horses to one pontoon wagon and they could not budge it. So they took a company of men and they drug them out to where the horses could get solid footing. There were about seventy-five Pontoons stuck and I'll bet it was no fool job a dragging them out. Some of the boys sang out and says we hant Soldiers any more, we are Burnside's mules. I thought so myself about that time." — Private John J. Laughton, Co. E, 15th NJVI, to a friend, from camp near White Oak Church, VA, 2/9/63 (John Laughton Letters, John Kuhl Collection)

Sergeant Lucien A. Voorhees, 15th NJ Volunteer Infantry (John Kuhl)

"…at dark, we…took up our line of march back for our old camp. And such a march! The renowned mud march of Burnside was no comparison to it. One day and night's rain had transformed the solid, dusty roads into complete sloughs, through which we floundered in the pitchy darkness. Now and then some man would lose his balance and tumble out flat in the deep mud, his gun flying out of his hands, taking him some time to find it and fish it out. We marched some four or five miles that night, crossing Robertson's river, and then encamped. During all this time, it had been steadily raining, increasing the depth of the mud." – Sergeant Dayton E. Flint, 15th NJVI, to his father, from camp, 2/7/64 (Dayton Flint Letters, John Kuhl Collection)

Private John Laughton, 15th NJ Volunteer Infantry (John Kuhl)

"Last night was cold. The ground froze hard, and there is ice in my tent. It will be beautiful today and then most likely will become muddy…" — Colonel Robert McAllister, 11th NJVI, to his wife, from Brandy Station, VA, 2/10/64 (Robertson, ed. *McAllister Letters*)

"Last night the Captain sent me to the landing with the mail and to bring up the mail. It is about seven miles distant by the road, and the road is despicable…I got there all right, but before I started back, it began to rain…My horse was very willing and he flew over the road till it became so muddy that he could hardly trot and then he suddenly plunged into a hole that took him up to the belly in mud and water…I very soon came to a place where a small by-path turned to the right, and as it seemed to me that by taking it, I should cut off part of the road…I dashed into it…and at last the horrible truth flashed across my mind that I was lost in the woods…Two hours of the most miserable riding…I was in sight of the shipping on the James River and must therefore have come back instead of going forward…" — Private James Horrocks, Batt. E, NJLA, to his father, from Bermuda Hundred, VA, 5/24/64 (Lewis, ed. *My Dear Parents*)

"A succession of dry, cold, clear days has baffled all calculations & reversed all experience. Frost six inches deep & uninterrupted pounding have given us fine roads for a week in succession, a thing heretofore unheard of in the history of the sacred soil…. How treacherous and impracticable this rebel soil and climate… 99 to 1 we will have the mud nineteen inches deep by tomorrow night." — Colonel Edward Martindale, 81st USCT, to his wife, from Virginia, 2/3/65 (Martindale Papers, Stanford University Library)

And so it went. And it was something that, many years after, in the GAR halls and local watering holes, they would never forget. As the years went by, the mud mayhap got deeper and more glue-like, but, like the war itself, it never left their imaginations.

Camp Vredenburgh
by
Dr. David G. Martin

Camp Vredenburgh, near Freehold, was established in July of 1862 as the assembly or rendezvous point for troops raised in the central part of the state of New Jersey (Monmouth, Ocean, Mercer, Middlesex and Union counties). President Lincoln had called for 300,000 more volunteers for three-years service, and in order to help fill its share of this quota the state decided to raise five new regiments of infantry, to be organized at five new camps established throughout the state. The regiment raised at Vredenburgh was the 14th New Jersey Volunteer Infantry, commanded by Colonel William Truex. The other three years' regiments enlisted in New Jersey that summer were the 11th, at Camp Perrine in Trenton; the 12th at Camp Stockton in Woodbury; the 13th at Camp Frelinghuysen in Newark; and the 15th at Camp Fair Oaks in Flemington. These camps would also be used to assemble other units for different terms of service in the next two years.

A campsite was selected about two and one-half miles west of Freehold, on the site of the Revolutionary War Battle of Monmouth. The camp was advantageously situated near running water (Spotswood Middle Brook), woods, and the Freehold and Jamesburg Agricultural Railroad. The site was especially praised for being "convenient of access from all parts of the district and just the right distance from the town for the comfort both of soldiers and citizens." (This meant that merchants could conveniently ply their wares near the camp, but rowdy or drunken soldiers would not have ready access to the town.) The land was leased from local farmer Jacob Herbert for approximately $34 a month during the two and one-half years it was open.

The camp, officially known as "Rendezvous No. 3," was named in honor of Peter Vredenburgh Sr., a prominent local judge (1805-1873) (the name is sometimes spelled without an "h" on the end). His son, Peter Vredenburgh, Jr., (born 1837) was soon elected major of the 14th Regiment, the first unit raised in the camp. Major Vredenburgh was detailed to a staff job for much of the first part of his enlistment, but then asked to be sent to the front with his command. He was killed in action in his first battle on September 19, 1864, while commanding his regiment at the battle of Opequon, Virginia (also called Third Winchester). He had just called to his men, "I will do all I can for you,

Peter Vredenburgh Jr. (Andrew M. Megill)

boys!" when he was hit in the neck by an unexploded artillery shell. He is buried in Maplewood Cemetery in Freehold. His military frock coat is on display at the Monocacy Battlefield Visitor Center outside of Frederick, Maryland.

Work on constructing the camp began on July 22, 1862. Large tipi-like Sibley tents were issued to the companies as they formed, while the officers lived in wall tents. A guardhouse, cookhouse, and railroad stop were erected, and a hospital was established. Local farmers were contracted to deliver fresh beef five days a week, in addition to wood and straw. These and other camp necessities (clothing, food and equipment) were issued by the acting quartermaster of the camp, Major William S. Stryker.

Men came to enlist singly and in groups. On August 14, 1862, a whole company of 105 recruits from Ocean County arrived in a great procession that included a band and 34 carriages. Daily life included drill and throngs of visitors. Sunday church services were provided in camp by ministers from Freehold's churches, including Reverend Taylor and Reverend Herr.

The campsite became more crowded in early August, when two more New Jersey units, the 28th and 29th regiments, were organized there. Because of a shortage of tentage, wooden barracks were constructed for the new regiments. Each barracks quartered about 100 men. Relations between the new regiments and the 14th were not always the best, because the men of the 14th had signed up for three years of military service, not the nine months contracted by the men of the 28th and 29th. The short-term recruits were often paid as much or more township bounty money as the men of the 14th. Questions of "patriotism" perhaps tinged with envy, brought on more than one fistfight at the bars in Freehold. Another untoward incident occurred in late August when a crazed soldier of the 14th stabbed his wife while returning to camp. There were also rumors of a Rebel spy operating in the camp.

On August 22, 1862, the 14th Regiment began preparations to leave for the war. All its men were ordered to be in camp that day for roll call and a parade. On Saturday, the men were assembled to receive their $25 down payment on $100 federal bounty (the remainder was paid on discharge). Sunday's events included a 3:30 P.M. service by Reverend Rose of Freehold. The regiment was officially mustered into United States service on August 26. A final dress parade in Freehold was held on August 31. The regiment's last night in camp was Monday, September 1, 1862 – a night marked by a severe rain storm that flooded the camp. On Tuesday morning, the men packed up their soggy gear and entrained for Philadelphia. The officers traveled in a passenger car, while the enlisted men had to ride in old baggage cars.

The 28th and 29th regiments continued training in Camp Vredenburgh for another month after the 14th left. The 29th was mustered into United States service on September 20, followed by the 28th on September 22. The 29th, commanded by Colonel Edward F. Applegate, left for Washington on September 28, followed by the 28th Regiment under the command of Colonel Moses N. Wisewell on October 4. The camp remained deserted for the next nine months until the 28th and 29th returned from Virginia. Both regiments, the 29th on June 28 and the 28th on July 6, were mustered out of the service at Vredenburgh.

The last unit raised at Camp Vredenburgh was Company H of the 35th New Jersey Volunteer Infantry, organized in August of 1863 under the command of Captain William Spain. Initially intended to be part of the 36th New Jersey Volunteer

Infantry, a unit that did not materialize when it failed to recruit enough men, the company was mustered in on September 24 and transferred to the 35th at Camp Fair Oaks in Flemington.

Camp Vredenburgh was closed in late January of 1864, when its buildings were dismantled and shipped to Trenton. Its drill fields were soon overgrown with woods, and its location was all but forgotten until 1983, when Dr. David Martin, working under a grant from the New Jersey Historical Commission, used oral tradition, contemporary literary evidence, and historic maps and deeds to establish beyond reasonable doubt that the Civil War training camp known as Camp Vredenburgh was located south of the Cobb House in Block 65, Lot 42 of Manalapan Township in Monmouth County. The site is fortunately preserved undisturbed within the confines of the current Monmouth Battlefield State Park. Test digs have uncovered a number of Civil War artifacts, sufficient to confirm the location of the site. A commemorative marker for the camp was erected nearby on Route 522 just west of the Cobb House on August 17, 1987, but there are no further plans being developed to investigate or interpret the site as of the date of this publication. (Martin, ed. *The 14th New Jersey: A Commemorative History*; Bilby and Goble, *Remember You Are Jerseymen*)

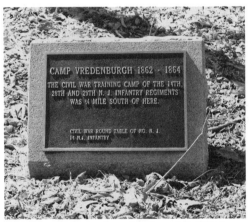

Camp Vredenburgh marker (Joseph G. Bilby)

Levi Van Zant and the 22nd New Jersey Volunteer Infantry
by
Thomas R. Burke

Levi Van Zant (also spelled Vansaun or Van Zandt) was born in New Barbadoes, (later known as Hackensack), New Jersey, on June 27, 1836. In 1858, Van Zant married Frances M. Outwater, and the couple subsequently had three children. The 1860 census reported 18 persons classified as slaves still residing in New Jersey, including 70-year-old Sarah Tompson, who resided in the household of Levi's father, Henry. To be a slave, or as the state classified it, an "apprentice for life," in 1860, Sarah would have to have been a slave on July 4, 1804, as New Jersey's abolition law classified all children of slaves born after that date as "apprentices" to be freed at the ages of 21 (female) and 25 (male). By 1846, remaining masters were legally obligated to support their remaining "apprentices" whether they continued in "apprenticeship" or were legally freed. Apprentices actually had the option of refusing manumission if it were offered to them.

Colonel Abraham Demarest, 22nd NJ Volunteer Infantry (John Kuhl)

Slavery in New Jersey had a long history, with the first enslaved people brought within what became the state's modern boundaries as early as 1623. The New Jersey slave population, some eight percent of the state's residents throughout the 18th century, reached its height in 1800, with 12,422 slaves recorded, the vast majority of them living in the northern part of the state. In 1804, with the urging of Governor Joseph Bloomfield, the New Jersey legislature passed the Gradual Emancipation Act, which mandated freedom for children subsequently born to slaves at the ages of 21(female) and 25 (male), while continuing the involuntary servitude of African-Americans already enslaved. Individual slave owners also occasionally liberated their slaves, regardless of age. An 1846 act abolished formal slavery altogether, relabeling persons still slaves as "apprentices for life," although the federal census apparently still classified them as slaves.

The presence of actual slavery in northern New Jersey no doubt added to the anti-war sentiment generated by fear of losing local industry's considerable

Southern markets with the outbreak of the Civil War. In July 1861, a peace meeting was held in Schraalenburg, and several hundred people heard Thomas Dunn English declare that the Lincoln administration had "betrayed a settled purpose to destroy the rights of the states and individuals." On September 5, 1861, United States marshals were dispatched from New York to Hackensack to pull down a Confederate flag hoisted by local Southern sympathizers. The men of the "American Guard," a Hackensack militia unit, protested the marshals' actions and were disarmed by the federal authorities.

The advent of war indeed resulted in severe unemployment in Hackensack and surrounding towns once Southern commercial ties were severed. Although the economy subsequently recovered, with new markets provided by federal military spending, anti-war sentiment remained high throughout Bergen County. This feeling was evident when New Jersey, presented with a federal demand to raise troops for nine-months service in the summer of 1862, established enlistment quotas for municipalities throughout the state. Bergen County's municipalities were held responsible for the majority of the men who would fill the 22nd New Jersey Volunteer Infantry. In order to fill quotas and avoid a state-sponsored draft in an area where anti-war feeling was fairly strong, local towns offered higher bounties to potential volunteers than any other municipalities in New Jersey. Some recruits collected as much as $325.

The bounties drew recruits. Although Levi Van Sant's wife was eight-months pregnant at the time, he and his younger brother Isaac enlisted in the 22nd's Company C on September 1, 1862. The company also recruited fifteen members of the American Guards, the unit previously disarmed by federal marshals, as well as men from the Continental Guards, another Hackensack militia unit not known for its pro-war spirit. Many of the rest of the regiment's volunteers, save the men of Company A, who were mostly Unionists and Republicans from Ho-Ho-Kus, held views of the conflict similar to those of the American Guards.

The 22nd's recruits were sent to Trenton, where they were reinforced by some Mercer County men, organized into a formal unit and given some rudimentary training. Officers from the regiment's ten companies elected Cornelius Fornet as the regiment's colonel and Alexander Douglas as lieutenant colonel. The selection of the foreign-born Fornet initiated what became a nine-month-long gripe fest by the 22nd's Bergen County anti-war faction, who characterized Fornet as a "foreign refugee" foisted on the regiment and not fit to command "the Democratic rank and file from Bergen County." The colonel resigned in disgust.

On September 29th, the 22nd left Trenton for Washington under the command of Lieutenant Colonel Douglas. The Jerseymen initially camped on East Capitol Hill but soon moved across the Potomac to build fortifications north of Georgetown, where they continued to gripe. The Emancipation Proclamation particularly annoyed some of the Hackensack boys, one of whom wrote the Bergen County *Democrat* protesting that he and his fellow volunteers were not ready for combat, "not that we are afraid to buckle on the shoulder straps, but because we do not believe in the cause." Not everyone in the regiment agreed and a writer to the Paterson *Guardian* protested that the men of the 22nd had joined the regiment, for significant bounties, to preserve the Union, and asserted that "the 22nd is loyal and brave…and when called upon will do its duty."

At the end of November, the regiment was provided with a chance to do its duty. Ordered to support General Ambrose Burnside's campaign against Fredericksburg, the men of the 22nd marched 80 miles in winter weather, slogging along through mud, rain, wind and snow, sleeping in shelter tents in the muck every night, until they reached Aquia Creek Landing, where they were assigned to load and unload supplies, transfer wounded men from railroad cars to steamships and guard Confederate prisoners.

In January 1863, the 22nd, much to the dismay of many of its men, was transferred to the First Army Corps, a battle-hardened front-line outfit with an excellent combat record. Twenty-three soldiers from Company C and a non-commissioned officer from Company A refused to move with the regiment, claiming they were insufficiently trained to be combat soldiers. After considerable argument, the 22nd marched off, leaving the protesters behind. A few days later the reluctant warriors did rejoin the regiment, no doubt chastened by threats of courts-martial and military-prison sentences at hard labor. The slacker Jerseymen rejoined their command just prior to General Burnside's "Mud March," where they pulled wagons and artillery pieces out of seemingly bottomless goo before going into winter quarters at Belle Plain, Virginia.

Lieutenant Colonel Douglas, unpopular with the anti-war crowd in the regiment, resigned his commission in January and was replaced by Abraham Demarest, who intensified the unit's drill schedule to ready the Jerseymen for combat. The 22nd was with the First Corps during the battle of Chancellorsville but was held in reserve until ordered to retreat under heavy enemy artillery fire. The regiment reported six men wounded during the withdrawal. For the next several weeks, the 22nd marched hither and yon around northern Virginia, until news of General Robert E. Lee's invasion of the North sent the Army of the Potomac in pursuit. The First Corps would engage in bloody fighting at Gettysburg on July 1, but the 22nd New Jersey would be elsewhere. As the Union army marched north, the 22nd's nine-month enlistment was about to expire, and when the regiment reached Centreville, Virginia, it left the army to return to New Jersey. The 22nd arrived in Trenton on June 22, 1863, and was discharged from federal service four days later.

Hackensack hosted a parade to welcome the returning Bergen County veterans. The political divisions within the regiment were so strong, however, that members of Company A refused to march in the parade along with the men of Company C, who they called "copperheads," a common name for Southern sympathizers. And this characteristic squabble provided the last line in the strange story of a New Jersey Civil War regiment better known for political infighting than fighting the enemy.

Private Levi Van Zant of copperhead Company C, 22nd New Jersey Volunteer Infantry, survived and came home to Bergen County. Interestingly, he later named one of his sons Robert Lee Van Zant. Levi passed away on May 24, 1904. His widow Frances was still living and listed as a "boarder" In the Hackensack home of Mae and Richard Van Kenson on the 1910 census. The stepfather of musician and actor Steven Van Zandt (born Steven Lento), longtime member of Bruce Springsteen's E Street Band and founder of his own band, Little Steven and the Disciples of Soul, as well as Wicked Cool Records, is a direct descendent of Levi and Frances, and Steven's brother Billy Van Zandt is an Emmy nominated playwright/producer/actor. In an ironic twist, Steven brought this unique Jersey story full circle, back to northern New Jerseyans fighting with each other, as he played Silvio Dante in the HBO series "The Sopranos." (Bilby and Goble, *Remember You Are Jerseymen*; Interview with playwright Billy Van Zandt; bit.ly/Van_Zant)

Levi Van Zant's grave in New York/Maple Grove Cemetery in Hackensack
(James M. Madden)

Panic on the Palisades
by
James M. Madden

Hiram Barney, Collector of the Ports of New York, petitioned the navy to protect New York Harbor. Barney was also a patron of the 54th New York Infantry, the unit that bayoneted Mayor Carpenter of Hudson City. (Library of Congress)

During the Civil War, many people living in northern coastal states, including New Jersey, had a decided, if in retrospect seemingly unreasonable, fear of Confederate naval attacks. New Jerseyans were familiar with stories of British coastal raids during the War for Independence, and the naval blockade with occasional enemy forays ashore in the state during the War of 1812, when the British also burned Washington, D.C., and attacked Baltimore's Fort McHenry. Although the Union navy dominated the high seas, the persistence of historical memory may well have been responsible for a willingness to believe the 1861 scare story that Confederate privateers were about to descend on Cape May.

By early 1862, there were other unpleasant possibilities, however. In early March, Confederate Navy Secretary Stephen R. Mallory anticipated that his new Confederate ironclad ship CSS *Virginia* might break out through the Union blockade of Hampton Roads, sail north around Sandy Hook, and "shell and burn... [New York] city and the shipping." Mallory predicted that "such an event would eclipse all the glories of the combats of the sea" and "strike a blow from which the enemy could never recover. Peace would inevitably follow." In actuality, of course, the Union ironclad ship *Monitor* sailed down from New York and stifled any possible threat from *Virginia* in a drawn battle fought on March 9.

That autumn, however, another danger arose, this time closer to home. The heavily armed Rebel commerce raider CSS *Alabama*, secretly constructed in England, commanded by Captain Raphael Semmes and manned by Southern officers and a European mercenary crew, was officially commissioned as a Confederate warship in August 1862. *Alabama* sailed towards the New England coast and then south, wreaking havoc on Union civilian shipping along the way.

One of *Alabama*'s victims, the old sailing ship *Baron De Castine*, had little actual value, but became a Confederate propaganda vehicle when Semmes dispatched it back to Boston along with 45 hapless prisoners from three destroyed merchantmen and a message to the New York Chamber of Commerce. Semmes advised the New Yorkers that he would soon be "prowling off the coast awaiting to pounce on Union shipping." He knew the story would spread rapidly through the Northern press and, if the local media needed any more prodding, *Alabama*'s crewmen had boasted to the prisoners that they were going to sail into New York harbor with guns blazing. Semmes captured and burned several merchant ships some 80 miles off the coast of New York and New Jersey in late October, and then, satisfied he had struck a moral blow at the commercial capital of the Union, the Confederate captain sailed off to the south, seeking more easy prey.

No one in New York knew Semmes had departed the area, however, and on November 7 the *New York Times*, responding to the perceived *Alabama* menace, complained about the decrepit condition of New York's harbor fortifications, noting that "the City was comparatively unprotected from the assaults of the enemy by sea." The existing forts, according to the paper, "would prove at best an uncertain and inefficient defense against swift-moving vessels." *Alabama*'s threats seemed genuine and the press continued to promote the idea that a Confederate seaborne attack could occur at any moment, which did nothing to calm public anxiety.

The harbor forts may have been in poor shape, but shipyard workers in Jersey City, Hoboken and Brooklyn were assiduously constructing warships that might actually provide a more effective response to an enemy naval assault. The most imposing of these, the "Stevens Battery," a massive 420-foot-long and 40-foot-wide ironclad ship designed by the Stevens family of Hoboken, had been an off-again, on-again work in progress for over two decades, but was, unfortunately, nowhere near ready to defend the harbor.

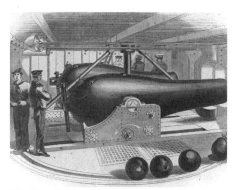

The *Passaic*'s two Dahlghren guns
(Harper's Weekly)

But the USS *Passaic* might be. The *Passaic*, a Brooklyn-built ironclad, was seaworthy and ready to test its cannons that fall, and the New Jersey Palisades cliffs seemed to provide the most convenient location for gun trials, as there was no danger of shot and shell caroming off into a densely populated local countryside. The navy picked November 15 as the test date, and on that crisp and cold autumn morning, the *Passaic* steamed out of Brooklyn and up the Hudson at a speed of seven knots, bucking a strong ebb tide and a heavy northerly wind. At noon, the ironclad anchored opposite Fort Lee, the highest point of the Palisades, some 200 yards from the shoreline.

Sailors loaded the ship's 15-inch Dahlgren gun, and aimed it at New Jersey. It misfired several times, to the amusement of those officers aboard who had predicted that the ship's turret design would interfere

The *Passaic*'s turret and wheelhouse
(Harper's Weekly)

The *Passaic* bombarding the Palisades at Fort Lee. (Harper's Weekly)

with effective gunnery. And then, on the fourth attempt, the Dahlgren fired. That first round splintered the rock wall and produced a massive echo that witnesses likened to the explosion of a powder mill. Despite the noise, the navy was satisfied, as there was no concussion or smoke inside the ship's gun turret, despite dire predictions from critics. Three more shots produced as many more echoes and showers of shattered rock. An Irishman aboard, awed by the destructive demonstration, declared the *Passaic* a "floating divil." All in all, *Passaic* turned in a spectacular performance after the initial misfires. Unfortunately, the officers in charge of the morning outing had not advised the local citizenry in advance.

Downriver, the *Passaic's* unannounced gun drill caused public tension to percolate into panic, as rumors ran rife that the Confederate navy, perhaps in the person of Captain Semmes, had indeed breached the defenses of New York harbor and that one or more Rebel warships were steaming up the Hudson River raking the New Jersey and New York shores with their artillery. People could hear reverberations of gunfire and the impact of solid shot and shells on stone as sound cascaded beyond the Palisades, and for some there could be no explanation other than a Rebel attack. It was some time before the truth got out and the fright subsided.

The *Passaic*, unwitting perpetrator of the panic, was Swedish-born John Ericsson's second ironclad design, a larger ship featuring heavier iron plating and bigger guns than his original *Monitor*. The new model also had better ventilation, higher smoke funnels, improved raft and hull shape, and a pilothouse atop the turret for better command and control. Even more importantly, its guns did not protrude outside the turret and were thus faster and easier to load.

This second generation Ericsson ironclad, named for a New Jersey city, county and river, gave its name to an entire class of similar ships. The initial *Passaic*-class "improved *Monitor*," built in the Brooklyn Navy Yard, was the first of ten of its type, two of which, including the USS *Weehawken*, were constructed by Zeno Secor & Company at the Jersey City shipyard of Joseph Colwell's Fulton Foundry.

Although the Confederate invasion scare was soon dispelled, the defensive weakness of New York harbor was still a real concern for many officials. Hiram Barney, Collector of the Ports of New York, petitioned the navy to permanently station *Passaic* in the area to compensate for the lack of decent harbor defenses. The navy had different priorities, however, and wanted to get its new model ironclad ships into action as soon as possible. *Passaic*, followed by her sister ships, as fast as New York and New Jersey shipyards could crank them out, headed south to reinforce the blockading squadron. On the way, *Passaic* and her crew received a personal visit from President Lincoln while docked at the Washington Navy Yard. The *Passaic*-class ironclads played a significant role in naval operations for the rest of the war, and the design proved so successful that later versions would be built for the Imperial Russian navy.

From that day in mid-November 1862 through the end of the Civil War, the Palisades at Fort Lee, New Jersey, was a naval artillery target range and proving ground for the guns of all the ironclad ships built in Jersey City and Brooklyn. The local citizenry got used to the noise, and took it in stride, as the possibility of Confederate naval action against New York City waned, even from active imaginations. Ironclad vessels changed the future of warfare at sea. Jersey City shipyards built them, and the cliffs of the Palisades played the vital role of target backstop, all as part of New Jersey's significant contribution to saving the Union. (Church, *John Ericsson; Harper's Weekly; Illustrated Times of London; New York Herald; New York Times*; Gaines, *Encyclopedia of Civil War Shipwrecks*; Semmes, *Memoirs of Service Afloat*; Spann, *Gotham at War*; Welles, *Diary of Gideon* Welles)

Religious service aboard the *Passaic*. Note racially integrated crew. (US Navy Historical Center)

Peaches
by
S. Thomas Summers

The Peach Orchard
Longstreet charges Sickles' Line
Gettysburg: July 2, 1863

Before the Johnnies arrived, I found myself trying
to fill my nose with the sweet smell of peaches –
close as we were to an orchard.
Dozens of them hung from the trees

like little green bells. Guess they needed
more time to grow. Newark doesn't smell
like sugar, all brick and factory,
so I dreamt those peaches were ripe and bleeding

sugar all over me, but then Rebs barreled
through that orchard, snapped me
from my thoughts like a baby from a nap.
Battle haze started choking air and lung.

Lead hummed by my head like pestered flies –
Now, the Rebs didn't want peaches.
They were after the artillery I was charged
with firing.One Reb got so close that I heard

him yell *Give us dem guns*. So I screamed back
Come and get'em, but in my mind
I was defending peaches. We would

have done a better job too, but men were tripping
on shot up horses. One horse was squawking
like an old maid scolding us all
for not playing nice, but it shut its snout

and died soon enough. We fought a while,
and the Rebs never got my guns,
but I bet those bastards battered up
that orchard just to rile my spirit.

A man wants what he wants,
and, by God, I wanted them peaches.

Scene of Battery B's fight at Gettysburg.
The battery fired 1,342 rounds in the
"artillery hell" near the Peach Orchard
on July 2, 1863, burning out the vents of
two guns and saving them all from
capture. (Henry F. Ballone)

"They Did New Jersey Proud"
The 11th New Jersey Volunteer Infantry at Gettysburg
by
Joseph G. Bilby

As with other Yankee soldiers heading north that high summer of 1863, the men of the 11th New Jersey Volunteer Infantry were happy to cross over from Virginia into Maryland, where food and friendliness provided a stark contrast with the barren and hostile Virginia countryside they left behind. One soldier wrote, "we seem to breathe a new atmosphere, and the men are full of hope and courage."

They would soon need both. At 1:00 A.M. on July 2, 1863 the 11th New Jersey went into camp several miles south of Gettysburg, Pennsylvania. Arising at dawn, the regiment fell into the III Corps line, which extended south along Cemetery Ridge. During the course of the morning, Major General Daniel Sickles, Third Corps commander, considered the lay of the land to his front, and made a crucial decision to move his corps forward toward the enemy. Gettysburg is a hub, with spoke roads radiating north,

The 11th's Gettysburg monument stands near the Emmitsburg Road, where the regiment began its fighting withdrawal on July 2, 1863.
(Henry F. Ballone)

south, east and west. One of these, the Emmitsburg Road, runs south to Maryland, and it was towards this road that Brigadier General Andrew A. Humphreys' Second Division of the Third Corps of the Army of the Potomac advanced in line of battle on the sultry Thursday afternoon of July 2.

The division's three brigades, which included five New Jersey regiments, moved forward in perfect alignment as if on parade. It was a magnificent sight that remained fixed in the memory of witnesses long after the ensuing horror had faded. An officer of the battle-hardened Irish Brigade stood mesmerized by the advance until his reverie was broken by puffs of smoke in the woods to the west and artillery shells bursting over the heads of the marching men.

The soldiers of the 11th New Jersey advanced through the sporadic air bursts and took up a position fronting on the Emmitsburg Pike, extending General Sickles' dogleg Third Corps line to the north. Shortly after the Jerseymen deployed, ominous rumblings of artillery and the crackling of small arms fire arose to the south, causing a gunsmoke haze to rise above the trees to their left. A barrage of shellfire soon broke over them and they hugged the earth and grit their teeth while awaiting the inevitable infantry assault.

The sounds of firing grew heavier when Brigadier General Barksdale's Mississippi Brigade slammed into the federal salient in the Peach Orchard to the south. As wounded men and stragglers passed to the rear, the 11th rose, changed front and faced left, in order to protect the Second Brigade's flank.

Colonel Robert McAllister ordered his men to lie down again in line of battle as the artillery fire increased. The enemy fire, directed primarily against the Union batteries along the Pike, filled the air with exploding spherical case shot, anti-personnel ammunition showering shrapnel balls and shards of iron hither and yon, as well as solid shot, which was intended to dismount Yankee guns, bouncing and careening along the ground like deadly bowling balls.

As Barksdale's victorious Rebels emerged from the orchard in the distance, driving routed federals before them, McAllister ordered his men to rise. They stood two-ranks deep in an open field, the shell bursts now accompanied by random Minie balls, and awaited the onslaught. The noise soon reached a crescendo, and explosions mixed with the screams of wounded men. As the Jerseyans prepared to meet the Mississippians, their problems were compounded as another enemy brigade, Brigadier General Cadmus Wilcox's Alabamans, marched to the attack out of the fringe of woodlands to the west. The tempo of bullets zipping above and through the regiment's lines increased.

Colonel Robert McAllister commanded the 11th NJ Volunteer Infantry at Gettysburg and was wounded early in the action. (John Kuhl)

Major Philip Kearny, namesake nephew of his late famous uncle (who did not think highly of him), placed his hand on regimental adjutant John Schoonover's shoulder and said, "I tell you we are going to have a fight." He then spun like a top ten feet backwards with a Minie ball in his knee. The wound would prove fatal. The adjutant had Kearny carried to the rear, then ran along the line to find Colonel McAllister as the regiment, firing by rank, cut loose with a blaze of fire from its assortment of muskets, .69 caliber smoothbore Springfield Model 1842s and .58 caliber Enfield and Springfield rifle-muskets. Schoonover found the colonel down, with a case shot ball in his left thigh and his left foot gashed by a shell fragment. After seeing McAllister to the rear, the adjutant passed command to senior Captain Luther Martin. The 11th would go through three more commanders within the next half hour.

The 11th New Jersey was ordered to withdraw and fell back in line of battle. While other regiments broke and ran that day, the Jerseyans of the 11th contested every foot of ground and leaked casualties with every yard they yielded. Beset on front and flanks, the regiment gradually retreated towards Cemetery Ridge, a half mile to the rear, stepping over and around dead men and shattered equipment. At one point, with most of their officers down, the 11th's men wavered, but Captain William Lloyd, blood streaming from a wound, pushed to the front and rallied them and they continued their orderly retreat. Finally, as the decimated outfit began to fragment again, Union reinforcements sapped the momentum of the enemy assault which, after lapping the base of Cemetery Ridge, finally receded. At the end of that terrible day, Captain Samuel Tucker Sleeper, a tailor from Shrewsbury and one of the few officers of the 11th still on his feet, found himself in command of what had once been a fine fighting regiment.

The 11th New Jersey Infantry paid dearly for its constancy on the field at Gettysburg. Of the 275 officers and men the regiment brought to the Emmitsburg Road, 38 were killed outright or died of their wounds. Another 109 were wounded and 12 were missing in action. Their conduct was perhaps best summarized by Gettysburg scholar Harry W. Pfanz, who wrote, simply and truly, "They did New Jersey proud that day." (Adapted from Bilby and Goble, *Jerseymen*)

"Send for Calhoun"
A Surgeon's Story
by
Robert F. MacAvoy

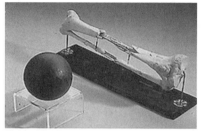

Sickles' leg bone
(National Museum of Health and Medicine)

"Place a guard around me, send for Calhoun, and don't let anyone operate till Calhoun arrives." So said General Daniel Edgar Sickles on July 2, 1863, as he was being carried from the field at Gettysburg with his lower right leg mangled by a glancing blow of a cannon ball.

James Theodore Calhoun was born at Rahway, New Jersey, on September 17, 1838, and began studying medicine at the age of sixteen under Rahway's Doctor Samuel Abernathy. Calhoun worked with Abernathy and several other doctors on a study to seek the cause of malaria in their small industrial town, determining that the disease was carried by stagnant water ponds created by Rahway River mill dams. Calhoun's research did much to encourage the legislature to pass a law removing the dams. Once the river ran free, the local health improved dramatically.

Calhoun graduated from the University of Pennsylvania Medical School in 1859 and established a practice in Rahway. He was commissioned assistant surgeon in the 5th regiment of the Excelsior Brigade, otherwise known as the 74th New York

A re-creation of the amputation of General Sickles' leg. (1) Dr. Calhoun operating surgeon; (2) Dr. Winslow; (3) Dr. Stone, anesthetizing. (Inset: Dr. James Theodore Calhoun) (*Journal of the Medical Society of NJ*)

Infantry, in June 1861. Although nominally a New York outfit, many of the brigade's men were Jerseyans. Calhoun distinguished himself as a surgeon early on, and was present for most of the Army of the Potomac's major battles. He performed hundreds of operations, including removing General Sickles' mangled leg, and in late 1864 was appointed surgeon-in-charge of Ward U.S. Army Hospital in Newark, New Jersey.

Calhoun married Nora C. Orr on May 3, 1865, and the couple had one child, a son, born in February 1866. After Ward Hospital closed in September 1865, he remained in the army, serving as medical director of transportation for the city of New York and post surgeon on Hart's Island in New York Harbor. In the summer of 1866, a cholera epidemic struck New York, and sixty-eight deaths were attributed to the disease by mid-July. On July 19, Calhoun stated that he was tired, nervous, and suffering from diarrhea. He began to vomit and died within hours. Sadly, his son Charley died of the same disease nine days later.

Calhoun was buried on Hart's Island, but was disinterred in February 1867 and reburied, along with Charley, atop a hill in Rahway's Hazelwood Cemetery in a ceremony with an honor guard of two infantry companies and a band. Flags flew at half-mast on Hart's Island and in Rahway, and business was entirely suspended in the town. (National Archives; Clark, *Medical Men of New Jersey;* English, ed. *Journal of the Medical Society of New Jersey*)

Calhoun's grave marker, Hazelwood Cemetery, Rahway (Diane MacAvoy)

Jersey Zouaves
"Scoundrels from New York and Philadelphia"
New Jersey's Zouave Regiments
by
Joseph G. Bilby

Captain Augustus Angel, a courageous Jerseyman, was killed in action in the Atlanta Campaign. (John Kuhl)

Captain Augustus Angel moved to subdue the mob, which his lackluster provost guard had allowed to run amuck. Drawing himself up to his full five feet six inches, the veteran officer approached two soldiers brawling in front of the stage depot and ordered them to cease and desist. Private William Egan, taking umbrage at the captain's presumption, swung at the officer. Egan's fist traced a clumsy drunken arc easily warded off by his sober opponent, who dropped him to the dirt with a counterpunch. Egan was up again in a flash, and clutching a drawn bayonet he attacked Angel, inflicting a bloody, if not serious, head wound. Stunned, the unarmed captain fell back before his aggressor, who moved in for the kill. A voice from the crowd cried, "Captain Angel, defend yourself!" And someone thrust the comforting butt of a revolver into Angel's outstretched hand. The captain knew what to do with a Colt, and cocking it, warned the advancing drunk, "Stop or I'll shoot." Egan lurched forward again and Angel fired, putting a ball through his attacker's heart.

As Private Egan lay dying in the dirt, his erstwhile companions in merriment cleared the streets, some scuttling back to Camp Parker to nurse their skinned knuckles, broken noses and throbbing hangovers, and others taking the high road to freedom, to enlist another day, in another place, for another bounty. Sheriff John L. Jones, Constable Reuben Paxson and their handful of deputies breathed a sigh of relief, although the town's purveyors of whiskey and cigars were, no doubt, somewhat dismayed.

Was the foregoing a scene from the lawless western frontier? Hardly. Angel and Egan were members of "Cladek's Zouaves," the 35th New Jersey Volunteer Infantry, and the shooting occurred in Flemington, New Jersey, on October 17, 1863. Another Zouave regiment, Colonel George W. Mindil's 33rd New Jersey Volunteer Infantry, was recruited in Newark. The popularity of the Zouave idea had its roots in the colorful French North African troops that made a name for efficiency and élan in the Crimean War and the campaign in Northern Italy in 1859. As elsewhere, Zouave militia units had sprouted in New Jersey like crocuses in spring in the wake of Elmer Ellsworth's Chicago Zouave Cadets drill team's 1860 national tour, and the state's three-months-service militia brigade sent to Washington in 1861 had its share of Zouave companies. These units imitated, to a greater or lesser degree, the uniforms and drill of their French namesakes. The 33rd and the 35th were, however, the only long-service Zouave units New Jersey fielded during the Civil War.

Private, Fatigue Uniform

STURCKE 74

Uniforms of the 35th NJ Volunteer Infantry, "Cladek's Zouaves," portrayed here in a Company of Military Historians print. (Roger Sturcke/CMH)

The regiments were recruited against a backdrop of desperation. The Enrollment Act of 1863 weighed heavily on New Jersey, where unmet troop quotas appeared likely to result in a draft. New Jersey's Governor Joel Parker beseeched the Lincoln administration to postpone conscription while he made an effort to fill the state's quota with volunteers. In the late summer and early fall of 1863, New Jersey proposed to raise infantry, cavalry and artillery units to beat the draft. Two of the infantry regiments were to be "Veteran Volunteer" Zouave outfits, intended, by their special uniforms as well as hefty bounties, to draw the cream of available recruits, especially those with prior service.

Many men drawn by the bounties were, like Egan, less than ideal soldiers. Although a local newspaper characterized the New Jersey recruit class of 1863 as "scoundrels from New York and Philadelphia," there were a fair number of home-grown scoundrels among them as well. Along with more than their share of scamps, however, the 33rd and 35th also enlisted a solid corps of veterans, especially officers. But, then as now, rogues and thugs made better press. In the end, somewhere between 200 and 300 Zouaves, up to a third of the regiment, each with approximately $300 of local bounty money in his pocket, "skedaddled" from the ranks of the 35th at Camp Parker.

"Zoo-Zoos" from the 33rd were taking their bounty money elsewhere as well, fleeing Newark's Camp Frelinghuysen with cash in their pockets, until Colonel Mindil called for reinforcements and was assigned the 3rd Vermont Infantry, fresh from the front. The Green Mountain boys gave the bounty jumpers second thoughts when they opened fire on a group of deserters fleeing across Roseville Avenue by moonlight, killing two of them.

Some Zouave officers were scamps as well; First Lieutenant Andrew Day and Second Lieutenant James McMillen "with force and arms broke and entered a certain building, a shanty…and threw down and totally destroyed said building…" The lieutenants helped themselves to the contents of the shanty, belonging to a sutler, and valued at $641.14. Both officers avoided the sheriff, but Day was brought to court in 1865. It is unclear whether or not Mr. Bryan, the aggrieved merchant, got his money back.

Needless to say, neighboring civilians were overjoyed to see both Jersey Zouave regiments leave for Washington, and when the 33rd departed in September, followed a month later by the 35th, desertions slowed down appreciably. Most of those who were going had already gone, and others, deprived of an easy jaunt to the fleshpots of New York City, became discouraged. William Lloyd, a sergeant in the 33rd, intended to leave the army as soon as he could, but wrote his wife Mary that he "wouldn't undertake it now under no considerations. There was 18 men caught in Washington this week that deserted from us."

Lloyd griped about marching up and down the "God damned hills of Virginia," but in late September the 33rd, along with the rest of the Eleventh Army Corps, was shipped to Tennessee to reinforce the federal army attempting to raise the Confederate siege of Chattanooga, and detailed to protect a pontoon bridge near Bridgeport, Alabama. The isolation there snuffed the last spark of skedaddle fever in Sergeant Lloyd, who ruefully informed his wife "there is no chance for desertion." He did, however, request that Mary send him belladonna, arsenic and other potions to enhance his chances for a medical discharge. She did not send them, perhaps afraid he might overdose. It would be a long war.

Captain Charles Courtois of the 33rd had a more upbeat view of army life. He insisted the 33rd was "the envy of the other regiments" on dress parade, and that one company raised regimental morale by singing "Johnny Fill Up the Bowl" and "imitating Roman candles on the march." (Just how they accomplished the latter feat went unsaid.) Courtois advised the homefolks in Paterson that it was "the duty of every loyal man to aid in arresting such rogues as Will Edsall," a deserter who had passed himself off as an officer to a number of gullible Jersey girls. The counterfeit "Captain" Edsall was finally arrested in June of 1864.

On November 23, the 33rd engaged the enemy for the first time. The regiment fought well, and drove its opponents from the field, losing one officer and one enlisted man killed and two officers and twelve enlisted men wounded. Following the Confederate defeat at Chattanooga, the Jerseymen participated in an arduous march to relieve Major General Ambrose Burnside's army, besieged in Knoxville.

The 35th New Jersey was also shipped to the western theater of war and, over the winter of 1864, was stationed in Kentucky, Tennessee and then Mississippi, where it served in Major General William T. Sherman's Meridian Campaign in February 1864. During the regiment's wanderings, Private Robert Conal of Company C, a veteran of nine-months service with the 21st New Jersey Volunteer Infantry, learned to hate General Nathan Bedford Forrest, noting that he would rather "have the gratifying pleasure of Hanging" the Confederate raider than sit down to an oyster dinner in Jersey City.

In the spring, the 35th was transferred to the Twentieth Army Corps and on May 4, 1864, both New Jersey regiments stepped off as part of General Sherman's drive on Atlanta. Private Martin Denniston of the 33rd wrote that "we marched all week, early and late," and that his "feet were sore and it was awfully hot." To mitigate his suffering, he threw away his "overcoat, woolen blanket, Zouave jacket and everything I did not need." He kept his musket, and would soon need that.

Colonel Mindil's regiment was the first Jersey Zouave unit to see action, when the 33rd was ordered to attack the defenders of Dug Gap, Georgia, while other Union troops outflanked them via Rocky Face Ridge. The Jerseymen scrambled up a steep embankment, regrouped behind some stone palisades and then charged alongside a New York regiment, dodging bullets and dislodged boulders to penetrate the Rebel line. Unsupported, they had to withdraw after dark. Colonel Mindil, bothered by an old wound, left the field and returned to Chattanooga, where he sat on an officer selection board, and then to New Jersey, where he spent much of his time lobbying the governor and the War Department to make him a brigadier general.

Mindil's regiment performed well without its colonel as the campaign progressed, however. At Resaca, Georgia, the Jersey boys "made a rush, yelling and hooting, guns roaring, bullets singing and whizzing around us," charging past the men of another unit who began "hollering 'Go in Jersies, we will follow you.'" That night the regiment, along with other troops, dragged four abandoned artillery pieces back to Union lines, the only guns the Confederates lost during the whole campaign.

Resaca was the 35th's first fight. After advancing under sporadic fire, the regiment assumed a defensive position, then, along with the 25th Wisconsin Volunteer Infantry, charged with "three rousing cheers" to relieve a Union force under heavy enemy pressure. After the Confederate evacuation of Resaca, Captain Angel led a two-company reconnaissance into the town and bagged thirty enemy stragglers and two sacks of Rebel mail.

Both regiments were actively engaged through the rest of the Atlanta Campaign. The 35th, under Captain Angel's tutelage, gained a reputation as fine skirmishers, fighting independently in front of the main battle line. On July 2, near a place called Ruff's Mills, Angel, now considered one of the best junior officers in Sherman's army, pushed his men within 70 yards of the enemy line, where he was shot. The bullet passed through the captain's heart and body, entered his arm and skidded down along the bone until it came to rest in his elbow. Seventy years later his grandson still had the misshapen slug, dug out of Angel after his death.

The Jersey Zouaves pushed deeper into Georgia, with steadily rising casualties, fighting at places with names never heard of back home, like Pumpkin Vine Creek, New Hope Church and Allatoona Creek. Sergeant Lloyd wrote his wife that "we suffer terrible, but I hope to God this thing will soon be over." And then they came to Atlanta.

On the late afternoon of July 20, 1864, Lieutenant Colonel Enos Fouratt advanced the 33rd to a small knoll about 500 yards in advance of the Union lines, where he deployed skirmishers and ordered the rest of the regiment to stack their weapons and begin collecting fence rails to prepare a defensive position. As the Jerseymen worked, a large enemy force, the leading element of General John Bell Hood's attempt to drive off Sherman's army, appeared out of the woods to their front. The Rebels fired a massive volley at the scattered soldiers of the 33rd and charged. Fouratt hastily formed the regiment into line of battle and attempted to make a stand, only to discover he was outflanked on the left and right, and then told his men to break and run for the main Union line. Miraculously, most of them made it, although they lost their state flag in the chaos. The 33rd reorganized and fought well in what would become known as the battle of Peach Tree Creek. The 35th was attacked in another of Hood's offensives on July 28. The Jerseyans fought from behind a barricade of logs and rails and cut down waves of Confederate attackers, losing only five men wounded.

Atlanta was now besieged. For the following month the Jersey Zouaves labored in hot, dusty trenches. And then, with Sherman's supplies running low, the Union general took most of his army on a wide flanking movement to cut the last railroad into the city, causing Hood to abandon Atlanta and end the grueling campaign. On September 2, with the returned Colonel Mindil at their head, the survivors of the 33rd New Jersey marched into Atlanta and camped in the captured city. Out of the 526 men the regiment began the campaign with, less than 200 remained. The 35th, which had lost 17 men killed, 80 wounded and 41 missing since May, settled into camp outside Atlanta. On September 14, the 33rd, its unique uniforms worn to a frazzle, adopted standard army garb, giving the remains of its Zouave clothing to the 35th, although the latter's uniforms were of a slightly different pattern. Both units shared several-hundred replacements, who arrived in Atlanta over the next month.

In mid-November, the Jersey Zouave regiments left Atlanta for Sherman's "March to the Sea," as his army, living off the land, cut a sixty-mile-wide swath across Georgia to Savannah. Many men, despite orders to do otherwise, used the occasion to appropriate whatever private property took their fancy. Sergeant Lloyd managed to "dig up out of the ground" a "silver chalice" some fleeing clergyman had buried for safekeeping. Although the march was mostly a carnival for the Jerseymen, the 35th ran into scattered resistance in early December and lost a corporal killed and several men wounded by a "torpedo" (land mine). To avoid future incidents, the Zouaves forced Rebel prisoners to clear the road in front of them.

On December 21, the 33rd triumphantly entered Savannah, camping in the heart of the city. On January 1, 1865, Sergeant Lloyd wrote his wife that "last night I had plenty of whiskey, but today I have none, we had five canteens full and we had a merry old time. They broke all my furniture and tore my table cloth and turned everything upside down. I thought I would fire a salute, I got my musket and fired it, and it set my tent on fire, and by the time I got through my tent was most burnt up. New Years comes but once a year & tents are cheap."

Within days the 35th was on the march again, the 33rd following at the end of the month. Sherman drove north into the Carolinas, with both regiments fighting the elements more than the Rebels, who steadily retreated. The Jerseymen felled trees to "corduroy" roads through the mud, destroyed enemy railroads and burned cotton and military supplies until the Confederate army to their front surrendered on April 26. And then they marched north to Washington. By the standards of Sherman's army, it was a cakewalk.

There would be a parade, a grand review in the capital, for a final look at one of the best armies the United States ever fielded. From a rocky beginning the Jersey Zouaves had turned into two of the finest fighting regiments in that army. Colonel Mindil finally got his stars – brevet promotions to brigadier and major general. Sergeant Lloyd, now a brevet second lieutenant, was thinking about moving to New York and getting a good job "on the cars" with his brother in law. And with that they marched off into history. (Bilby and Goble, *Jerseymen*; McAfee, *Zouaves*; Zinn, *Mutinous Regiment*; Lloyd papers. This essay is based on an article by the author in *Military Images Magazine*.)

"Excellent discipline and good soldierly qualities"
The 22nd United States Colored Infantry
by
Joseph G. Bilby

Colonel Joseph Barr Kiddoo, who commanded the 22nd US Colored Infantry until be was badly wounded in October 1864 in a controversial action at Fair Oaks, VA. (Jeffrey Mosser/USAMHI)

The 22nd United States Colored Infantry was organized at Camp William Penn, outside Philadelphia, in January 1864. With 681 New Jerseyans in the ranks, the 22nd was the most "Jersey" of all United States Colored Troops outfits. The regiment, under the command of Colonel Joseph B. Kiddoo, left for Virginia at the end of January and was assigned to General Benjamin Butler's Army of the James at Yorktown, where it drilled, trained and worked on fortifications.

The 22nd often marched through Williamsburg. One officer reported that the nondescript and seedy former Virginia capital was "a half mile long and seemed to have only one street." When a black regiment swung down that street, however, with fifes shrilling and drums tapping, it magically came to life, lined with cheering and dancing local African-American civilians.

In March, the 22nd supported Brigadier General Judson Kilpatrick's failed plan to liberate Union POWs in Richmond, marching thirty-three muddy miles to escort Kilpatrick's sodden and demoralized cavalrymen to Yorktown. Not a single man fell out of the regiment's ranks during the march, and an officer noted: "I wish I could tell all our 'Anti-colored soldiers' friends at home something of the haughty, proud doggedness, with which these brave fellows marched through mud, cold and rain, and some of them almost bare footed as their shoes were literally torn apart by the thick clay."

In May, the regiment gained praise as "well prepared for any attack of the enemy, and equal to any emergency that is likely to occur...." After Butler's march on Richmond failed at Drewry's Bluff that month, he withdrew his army into the vicinity of Bermuda Hundred. The Army of the James advanced again on June 13, however, in support of the Army of the Potomac's move towards Petersburg, a vital rail center south of Richmond.

On June 15, 1864, the 22nd, as part of the Eighteenth Army Corps, advanced on Petersburg. The regiment successfully overran a Confederate forward trench line at Baylor's Farm, suffering its first combat casualties of the war. At around 11:00 A.M., the corps came up against "the Dimmock Line," a series of earthworks surrounding Petersburg and manned by Confederate regulars and militia. General William F. "Baldy" Smith, the corps commander, conducted a lengthy reconnaissance of the position before ordering an attack. At sunset, the 22nd assaulted Battery Number Seven, a position defended by both artillery and infantry. Half the regiment, deployed in a loose "skirmish" formation to lessen casualties, circled to the left and infiltrated the Rebel rear through a gap in the defenses while the regiment's remaining men sprinted for the Confederate fort as fast as they could to get "under the guns", where the enemy artillery barrels could not be depressed enough to hit them. On arrival, however, they found their skirmishers already in possession.

The 22nd US Colored Infantry storms the Confederate lines at Petersburg.
(*Frank Leslie's Illustrated Newspaper*)

The black Jerseymen were immediately fired on from nearby Battery Number Eight, and Colonel Kiddoo ordered his men to charge that position. Captain Albert Janes led Company A, followed by the rest of the regiment, through a narrow swampy ravine swept by "a storm of leaden hail" and up a fifty-degree hill obstructed by brush. The 22nd's color sergeant, James Woby of Allentown, miraculously missed by a blizzard of bullets, led the assault, spinning around and waving his flag to encourage his comrades. Kiddoo recalled that his men, "seeing their colors on the opposite side of the ravine, pushed rapidly up" after Woby. The enemy beat a rapid retreat, leaving the fort to the bloodied and battered black troops.

Captain Janes, who lost five men killed and nine wounded of the seventy-eight he took into combat, wrote home that evening, after the whole Rebel defensive line had crumbled, that his men were "going to whip these rebs beautifully soon."

The regiment left a trail of eleven dead and forty-three wounded soldiers on its way to victory. Among the dead were Jerseymen Henry Brooks, Henry Johnson, Charles H. Conover, William Davis, William Grant, Thomas Price and Charles Young. One black sergeant was found alongside a Rebel sergeant — the two had bayoneted each other to death. The 22nd's total casualty list that day was 143 men killed and wounded. An official report praised the "men of the 22nd Regiment," noting that "to this regiment belongs the chief credit of this affair." A white reporter who witnessed the attack wrote that "the colored troops…won for themselves a fame which will have a record among the many splendid achievements of the Union army."

Unfortunately, General Smith halted the attack short of complete success, and his delay gave the Confederates time to reinforce Petersburg. As summer slipped into autumn, the Jerseymen of the 22nd endured the dreary danger of siege warfare, living a subterranean life sloshing through foul-smelling muddy trenches and dodging sniper bullets. Over the next ten months, Grant lengthened and weakened the Confederate lines by threatening their flanks. One of these operations got the men of the 22nd out of their trenches and on the march towards New Market Heights.

The Confederate defenses on the Heights had been unsuccessfully attacked twice before by white troops, and this time General Butler decided to give his black soldiers a chance. When the African-American division attacked New Market Heights on September 29, 1864, the 22nd, led that day by Major J. B. Cook, was deployed on the division's left flank. Troops to the regiment's right were halted and driven back but then surged forward again. The 22nd forced its way through thickets and a swamp under heavy fire, and drove to the New Market Road behind the Confederate trenches as the enemy defense collapsed. The Jerseymen wheeled left and cleared the road, sweeping fleeing Confederates before them, then held off a counterattack. The little victory did not come without cost, however, and the 22nd lost six men killed in action and sixty-eight wounded. Among the dead were Privates Joseph H. Brown and Robert C. Goldsborough, both Jerseyans.

October 27, 1864, found the regiment at Fair Oaks, moving on a dismounted Confederate cavalry unit dug in along the Williamsburg Road. Unfortunately, Colonel Kiddoo led the attack in the wrong direction, and seven of his officers later alleged that the colonel, whose mood that day fluctuated between elation and panic, was drunk and that his confusing orders were "the sublime views and plans of a whisky-crazed brain." The confusion was exacerbated when Kiddoo was badly wounded, and compounded by the fact that a number of new, barely trained recruits in the ranks panicked when they received flanking fire from Confederate skirmishers.

Although most of the 22nd's bewildered troops stood fast or fell back, some charged the enemy with another regiment and captured several artillery pieces before being driven back by enemy reinforcements. The men of the 22nd who fought at Fair Oaks fully sustained their regiment's reputation. John Loveday, the Jerseyman first sergeant of Company A, refused attention when badly wounded, instead urging his men forward in the attack. Color-bearer Corporal Nathan

Stanton was another heroic Jerseyan who, although wounded, continued to carry the regimental flag. Yet another New Jersey soldier, First Sergeant William F. Robinson of Company E, was cited as "especially distinguished for gallant conduct." The regiment lost one officer and four men killed and forty-four men wounded before the Jerseyans slogged through rain and mud back to their starting point, ending what one officer called a "grand fizzle."

In December, the regiment was assigned to the new Twenty-fifth Corps, the only all-black army corps in United States military history. The soldiers of the 22nd remained in the trenches before Richmond through spring, dodging bullets and shells and fighting lice and rats as well as Rebels. In February, the regiment, recovered from the fall campaign, well-drilled

Jerseyman Sergeant Edward Richardson, Company A, 22nd US Colored Infantry, and friend (USAMHI)

and disciplined, marched in review and conducted a complicated series of maneuvers before its commanders. African-American war correspondent Thomas Morris Chester was thrilled by the sight and took the occasion to refer to the 22nd as "among the best in the service."

On April 2, a massive push cracked the main Confederate line. As the Rebels fled Richmond the following day, the men of the 22nd were among the first Union infantrymen to enter the city, where they immediately went to work extinguishing fires set by retreating Confederates. Following General Robert E. Lee's surrender and the assassination of President Abraham Lincoln, the 22nd, chosen "on account of its excellent discipline and good soldierly qualities," was ordered to Washington to participate in Lincoln's funeral procession. Afterward, the regiment was deployed on Maryland's Eastern Shore as the army hunted John Wilkes Booth. Color Sergeant Woby recalled that "the men of the regiment were extended out in a long line with a space of several yards between each other, and that the country and buildings were thoroughly searched."

Following Booth's death, the men of the 22nd no doubt thought their war was over. Unfortunately, there was yet another dirty job to do for the black soldiers of the Twenty-fifth Corps who, with thousands of other troops, were shipped to Texas to intimidate the French-supported Mexican regime of "Emperor" Maximilian, as well as pacify the former Confederate state. The 22nd patrolled the border along the Rio Grande through October 1865, then returned to Philadelphia to be mustered out of service.

Although in combat less than a year, the 22nd lost two officers and seventy enlisted men killed in action or mortally wounded. One officer and 144 enlisted men died of disease. The regiment served New Jersey and the nation as well as the best of its white state-designated regiments. (adapted from Bilby, *Freedom to All;* Bilby & Goble, *Remember You are Jerseymen*)

The 22nd US Colored Infantry was the only black regiment to march in Abraham Lincoln's funeral parade. (National Archives)

Death and Lieutenant Colonel Davis: A Jerseyman's Journey
by
John G. Bilby

It was early morning on May 12, 1864. It had been raining for several hours, turning the ground at Spotsylvania into a morass. An early morning fog enveloped the Union troops moving forward, first at a walk and then at a run, up and over the initial Confederate emplacements. Soldiers slipped, fell, and then regained their footing as they surged forward, following Lieutenant Colonel Thomas H. Davis with an implacable momentum, driven onward through the fog. Davis, a native of Camden, New Jersey, was at the head of the 12th New Jersey Volunteer Infantry, *his* regiment, spurring his soldiers onward. His shrapnel wounds from the battle of the Wilderness, although superficial, were only three-days old. Now, at Spotsylvania, the regiment cleared the initial line of Confederate entrenchments, faced little resistance,

Lieutenant Colonel Thomas Davis, 12th NJ Volunteer Infantry (John Kuhl)

and moved forward. Davis was atop a second line of entrenchments, revolver in hand, when a round ripped through his throat and he fell dead off the berm. His soldiers fell back in confusion and disorder. The war was over for Lieutenant Colonel Davis. He was twenty-eight years old.

The war continued for Davis's family. They requested that his body be returned home to Camden. Thomas's mother, an aging widow, could do nothing, but Thomas's brother Lemuel worked tirelessly to retrieve his body. Lemuel was a talented man, an engineer who had made fortunes in Toledo and Detroit. Thomas had demonstrated a deep attachment to his brother, and followed him west. Lemuel would respond in kind, following his brother south after his death. He would journey to battlefields and engage politicians, all the way up to President Lincoln, in his effort to secure a final, decent burial for Thomas.

Thomas's family must have been deeply aggrieved, because he had not died the Victorian "Good Death." There were no last words to comfort his family, and he had failed to display any deep sense of religious faith. His strongest connection seemed to have been with his older brother, Lemuel.

Often, families sought comfort in condolence letters from the peers of their soldier, but there were none forthcoming from the battered 12th. Thomas was the last in a line of highly esteemed officers in the regiment and his death marked the passage of an era. He had been with the 12th from its inception, and the soldiers had been proud to claim him as their leader and appreciated his paternal dedication to their welfare. The 12th had lost 70% of its soldiers between Chancellorsville, a year prior, and Spotsylvania. Few officers remained, and none could summon the same kind of visceral, emotional response that Thomas did. No subsequent unit commander would be able to approximate the bond the regiment had with Davis. And his men would mythologize him until the end of the war – and beyond.

The Civil War marked the rapid industrialization of death and delivered it with speed and efficiency. This frightening upheaval magnified the importance of dying properly, because "dying was an art, and tradition had provided rules of conduct for the moribund and their attendants since at least the fifteenth century." Life on the battlefield offered a stark contrast to this tradition because it was often brutish, filthy, and unpleasant.

Battlefield burial was done quickly and usually poorly. The Spotsylvania battlefield was particularly chaotic and gruesome. The area where the 12th slammed into the Confederate lines was later known as the "Bloody Angle" because of the relentless combat that took place there. Thomas had died at the head of the advance; his men had fallen back and the Confederates had moved forward after he was killed. His body remained in the hands of his soldiers but was probably not buried until hours after his death. The weather was cool and wet; his body had not begun to swell as badly as the troops that died in the heat of summer. Still, Davis's fellow Jerseymen had been eager to bury him properly, and mark his grave.

Davis's family was fortunate because they knew of his fate and that somewhere he was in a marked grave. Lemuel Davis appeared in Fredericksburg on a pass from the provost marshal, Captain A.M. Wright, a week after Thomas's death. Fredericksburg was still a dangerous city on the front lines of the battle in northern Virginia. Moreover, the new bureaucracy of identification and graves registry had yet to catch up with the grieving brother. The Spotsylvania fight was barely over, and Davis's body was still somewhere in transit.

Lemuel returned home without his brother's body and contacted New Jersey State Senator James Matlack Scovell, a War Democrat who was an acquaintance of President Abraham Lincoln. On June 12, 1864, a month after Davis's death, Scovell sent a letter to Lincoln from Camden describing Davis's body's location as in "the neighborhood of Belle Plain." Belle Plain was the supply base for Lieutenant General Grant's Army of the Potomac, a "rude landing on the Potomac Creek... desolate in the extreme." It was nine miles east of Fredericksburg, and a site where the United States Sanitary Commission would off-load the dead.

The Sanitary Commission was the preeminent body for sorting and identifying Civil War dead. It was a philanthropic organization dedicated to the needs of soldiers, including hospital care, graveyards, registries of death, burials and, in the best of cases, shipment home. The Commission employed a network of agents in northern cities and authorized individuals to accept anticipated expenditures for body removal and return.

Early in the war, Northern states set the lofty goal of bringing every body home from the battlefield. The Sanitary Commission came to meet the needs of the deceased and their survivors after it became apparent that the confusion, chaos, and numbers were overwhelming the army. In the first year of the war, some units had taken up collections to send bodies home, a practice soon abandoned. Lemuel Davis, however, was determined to get his brother back, and he had the means to do so. Scovell noted in his letter to Lincoln that he "need scarcely add that the family of the deceased are among the oldest and most influential in West Jersey."

However, Thomas's body was not to be returned. Frederick H. Hall, a representative of Secretary of War Edwin M. Stanton, responded to Scovell that:

> [E]very facility that can be afforded to Mr. Davis to recover the body of his brother he shall have, but flags of truce are only granted by commanders in the field, and we have no officer now who can communicate with the enemy at Fredericksburg. There is therefore no method by which the body of Col. Davis can at present be obtained. If Mr. Davis desires a pass to go to Fredericksburg and run the risk of being captured, he shall have it.

The letter offered no options; Lemuel had already "run the risk" of capture a mere week after his brother's death. Belle Plain was firmly in Union hands and functioned as the supply depot for the Wilderness and Spotsylvania campaigns. However, supply depots generally provided slow-moving, high-value targets in the form of logistical supply trains, and Confederate guerrillas raided the area, harassing operations and attempting to inflict (mostly) psychological damage upon Union operations. The *New York Times* reported the capture of forty guerrillas halfway between Belle Plain and Fredericksburg in late May 1864, shortly before Davis's body arrived there.

Lemuel's relatively uneventful earlier visit, right after the particularly violent engagement at Spotsylvania, indicates that Hall might have been engaging in a bit of hyperbole. It is very likely that the War Office was flooded with requests, many from well-to-do families, for leave to retrieve the bodies of their loved ones. Civilians on the battlefield would create another distraction for busy commanders, especially in areas of intense guerrilla activity. Thus, it is understandable that the War Office would not actively support the intentions of many of the "oldest and most influential" families.

Lemuel was unable to retrieve his brother's body until November of 1865. The war had been over for six months and the country was just beginning to account for the deaths and disappearances of soldiers. The delay that year was caused by the summer heat, and Lemuel was one of the first to retrieve his brother's body; many less fortunate or well-off families waited until the winter of 1866 and beyond to learn of their loved one's location. For these families, the government took on the obligation to unearth and identify the dead, a service demanded by figures as well known as former New Jersey teacher Clara Barton and Camden resident Walt Whitman, who felt that the government owed it to its soldiers. Such emotional engagement in military death was unusual prior to the war, but killing on a massive scale had violently altered people's perceptions of what was appropriate regarding the dead. Lemuel was typical in this regard; he would brook no obstacles in his brother's recovery.

Lemuel received notification from the Assistant Quartermaster's Office that he could exhume and remove his brother's body on November 29, 1865, when he learned that Thomas was actually buried in the Fredericksburg City Cemetery, "on or about June 12/14 1864" – one month after he had initially tried to retrieve the body. He was told to furnish an "air-tight case and transportation for said body at your own expense." Wooden coffins had the potential to release the odors of decay and also fell apart upon prolonged exposure to the elements.

Airtight coffins became common towards the end of the war, advertised by embalmers, undertakers, and self-proclaimed agents who would retrieve bodies for families. One such entrepreneur was G.M. Scollay, who advertised a patented "metallic-lined, air-tight deodorizing burial case!" Scollay was a keen businessman with an eye for advertising; his card proclaimed that his caskets were "the cheapest and best way of preserving bodies during transportation." Scollay furnished Lemuel with a coffin and death certificate for transport of Thomas Davis, dated December 2, 1865. Lieutenant Colonel Davis was subsequently reburied in Laurel Hill Cemetery, Philadelphia.

Davis was fortunate to be identified and returned home, but his family had the means to retrieve his body. Many other families suffered for years after the war, lacking the psychological satisfaction of closure. Many longed for news of the Good Death of their loved one, a death faced bravely with patriotism and Christian piety. Many deaths, in fact, were just the opposite: anonymous and lonely, deranged with fever from wounds and infections, unaware of any sense of heavenly forgiveness for the things they had seen and done. (Davis Papers, Camden County Historical Society; Longacre, *Gettysburg and Beyond*)

"I Shall Have to get Married or be an Old Bachelor"
by
Diana B. Newman

While archiving Civil War research material as a volunteer at the National Guard Militia Museum of New Jersey in Sea Girt, I came across copies of a collection of letters by an officer in the 7th New Jersey Volunteer Infantry. His letters to his parents and siblings expressed fine sentiments in beautiful handwriting and I read them all, developing a relationship with this man I could never meet.

William James Evans was born on January 28, 1838, into an English family that emigrated to America and settled in Paterson. By the time of the Civil War, he had four sisters, Margaret, Elizabeth, Louisa, and Eliza. Margaret and Elizabeth were both married, and Margaret had two daughters of whom William was fond and called his "little nieces." William's father was a shoemaker and proprietor of a tavern. William was an engraver and volunteer fireman.

Captain William J. Evans, 7th NJ Volunteer Infantry
(John Kuhl)

In William's mind, being a volunteer fireman and a volunteer soldier went hand in hand, so, in September 1861, he and two fireman "chums" recruited a company of men that became Company G of the 7th New Jersey Volunteer Infantry. William became the company's second lieutenant. By February 1863, he had been promoted to captain, and commanded Company B of the 7th. He was modest about the captaincy, writing to his parents," Do not think for an Instant that owing to my Promotion I shall forget my Character as a man, or when I lead them in the Battle field I shall become exalted…." Showing a playful side, however, he wrote to Louisa, "I feel slightly elated myself…I may be a Colonel yet Ah! Ah! That would be a "Big Thing" Colonel Evans, just imagine…Aint You Proud of Your Big Brother eh?"

He and Louisa were so close that they asked each other for help finding marital matches. On March 25, 1863, he wrote to Louisa, "I have some very fine young men in my Company, and as you want me to pick you out a Beaux…come out here & choose one for yourself. What do you say to that?" On May 19, 1863, William asked his sister, "…have you found me a woman yet? No excuses accepted if you ain't… I shall have to get married or be an Old Bachelor, so I will leave it entirely in your Hands to save me from such a Dreadful Fate…." It appeared Louisa was successful. In a letter dated October 1, 1863, William wrote, "[R]elating to that beautiful Damsuel you have found for me, Oh she must be a Charming Creature as you say one of her legs (limb you ought to say) is a little bit shorter than the other, but that don't make any difference, You know I am blind of one eye but that don't make any difference. Oh what a happy pair we will make. Really I almost feel if I had wings, like soaring through the air to Paterson to view the charming creature with her 5 thousand dollars, Cottage &c… beg of her to remain single and wait till I came home… give her my kindest and unceasing love and a kiss for me…."

By the time I finished reading his letters, I had fallen in love with William myself, and wanted to know what became of him and his damsel, with her $5000 and cottage! And then I learned that he was killed at Spotsylvania and his grave was never found.

I cried. (Evans Papers, NJHS; Eckhardt and MacAvoy, *Our Brothers Gone Before*)

James Gorman's Tale
by
Robert F. MacAvoy

On August 19, 1861, the 6th New Jersey Infantry was mustered into United States service at Camp Olden in Trenton, New Jersey. In September, the regiment left the state with 38 officers and 860 noncommissioned officers and enlisted men, among them Private James Gorman of Camden County's Union Township and Company A. The 6th, along with the 5th, 7th, and 8th New Jersey Infantry, was organized into the Second New Jersey Brigade, which participated in major engagements at Williamsburg, Fair Oaks, Bristoe Station, Chancellorsville, Gettysburg and the Wilderness with Gorman in the ranks. In an assault at Spotsylvania, Virginia, on May 11, 1864, the brigade advanced on strongly held Confederate field fortifications, with the 6th New Jersey deployed in front of the line as skirmishers. In the course of that attack, James Gorman was badly wounded. He was evacuated from the battlefield to a field hospital at Sperryville, Virginia, where he died of his wounds on May 14, 1864.

There is a bizarre sequel to this sad story. On July 7, 1864, James Gorman was legally drafted into the service of the United States for a period of three years. The surviving notice from Captain Alexander Wentz, Provost Marshall of the First District of New Jersey, states, "You will accordingly report on the eighteenth day of July 1864, at the place of rendezvous, in Camden, N.J., or be deemed a deserter...." The notice emphasizes, "No further time will be allowed." Attached to the draft notice was a voucher for transportation from Gloucester City station to Camden on the West Jersey Railroad.

James Gorman's draft notice (National Archives)

Needless to say, James Gorman missed his reporting date at Camden, New Jersey, on July 18, 1864, but he kept his rendezvous with Grave #273, Terrace R, at Fredericksburg National Cemetery, Virginia. In his postwar report, Provost Marshal Wentz complained that the enrollment officers employed by his district, who were paid to register potential draftees on a per diem basis, were corrupt, in many cases enrolling those who were no longer residing in the district or deceased. The story of James Gorman certainly seems to support his complaint. (Bilby and Goble, *Remember You Are Jerseymen*; Draft Notice and Service Record of James Gorman, NA)

General Walker and the Jersey Surgeons
by
Valerie M. Josephson

John Joseph Craven (USAMHI/MOLLUS)

Newark's coroner, Dr. John J. Craven, served as a surgeon with the 1st New Jersey Militia in 1861. Following his three-month militia enlistment, Craven applied to the United States Army Volunteer Medical Corps and in October was appointed brigade surgeon to General Horatio Wright's brigade at Hilton Head. Within a year he was appointed chief medical officer of the Department of the South and then chief medical officer of the Departments of Virginia and North Carolina. Craven was with the Tenth Army Corps at Bermuda Hundred in Virginia when the campaign of 1864 began as General Benjamin Butler moved on Richmond and Petersburg. On May 20, Craven came across four Union soldiers and a corporal bearing a stretcher with a severely wounded Confederate officer. He recalled that:

> Something tempted me to halt and dismount. God forgive me if it was a desire to assure myself that all the suffering had not been on our side....His left arm was shot through; his right leg shattered and badly mangled above the ankle; his hip was torn by the fall of his horse, and life appeared fast ebbing.

Craven learned that the casualty was General William S. Walker. He gave Walker some brandy from a pocket flask and then scribbled a note to his hospital steward: "Take charge—will be with you soon." The doctor then galloped off to inspect the Tenth Corps hospitals. He did not return until midnight, and then determined that Walker's lower leg would have to be amputated immediately. There was insufficient light to operate, so Craven ordered some soldiers to tear down a nearby smokehouse and light a big bonfire. Before the surgery Walker, who believed he was going to die, hurriedly dictated two letters, one a farewell to his wife, Dora, and another to General P. G. T. Beauregard explaining how he was captured. The surgery was successful, however, and Craven kept Walker in his own tent until he was healthy enough to be moved to the general hospital.

Walker was a valuable prisoner and Craven bore a flag of truce to the enemy's lines with information on his condition in late May. The *New York Herald* reported that the Jersey doctor was received in the enemy lines by Walker's aide, one Captain Lowndes of South Carolina. Craven provided information on Walker's condition and prognosis and delivered a letter from the general. In return, Lowdnes provided information on some missing Union soldiers.

Walker was eventually transferred to Fortress Monroe, where he became the patient of another New Jersey doctor, contract surgeon David Warman of Trenton. Warman later recalled that Walker told him he had an aunt in Hoboken who had offered to "present him with an artificial leg if he would come on to New York." Although the general was denied a parole to go to New York, Warman agreed to make a plaster cast of his stump, which was "forwarded to the instrument maker" and used to make a prosthesis, presumably courtesy of the Jersey aunt. When the artificial limb arrived at Fortress Monroe, Warman fitted it to Walker and later noted that by the time the general was exchanged he "could walk almost as well as any of us." Walker's prosthesis was subsequently used as a model by the only company in the South to make such devices for Confederate soldiers.

(Eckerts, *Fiction Distorting Fact*)

The U.S. General Hospital at Beverly, New Jersey 1864-1865
by
William E. Hughes

  During the course of the Civil War, the state of New Jersey established a number of troop rendezvous camps where recruits were organized into regiments to be sent south. One of these camps was opened at the Burlington County waterfront town of Beverly. A number of units were mustered into the service at Beverly, including the 10th, 23rd, 24th, 25th and 34th New Jersey Volunteer Infantry regiments.

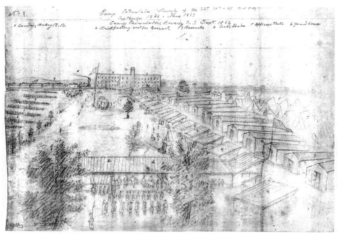

Camp Cadwallader at Beverly, 1862 (William E. Hughes)

  During the war, nearby Philadelphia became an important wartime medical center with a number of military hospitals. As casualties increased, especially during the bloody summer of 1864, the federal hospital system expanded. One account noted that "in the year 1864, the hospitals found they had many cases that were more or less permanent patients and a large extent cured but not well enough to go to their homes or to return to active duty, it was found necessary to establish convalescent hospitals at various points." As a result, Beverly became the site of a general hospital during the final year of the conflict. The same virtues that made the town an ideal rendezvous camp made it an attractive hospital location. Situated on the eastern shore of the Delaware River, about fifteen miles north of Philadelphia and only a few miles south of Burlington City, New Jersey, Beverly was a convenient destination point for both men and supplies, as it was readily accessible by Delaware River steamboats and the Camden & Amboy Railroad.

  By 1864, military doctors had determined that patients housed in tents often recovered more rapidly than those treated in permanent hospital buildings, and so the hospital itself, a large brick structure with previous service as a factory, was surrounded by exterior wards composed of tents accommodating eight to twenty patients each. The August 6, 1864, edition of the *Philadelphia Inquirer* reported that the "the new military hospital at Beverly is now ready for the reception of patients. The building is located in a healthy and delightful part of the above named place, and is capable of accommodating about 800 patients."

Soon after it opened, the hospital began to receive a steady stream of wounded men. Some casualties came to Beverly by train, but the majority arrived on steamboats that docked at the foot of Broad Street, with arrivals announced by the distinctive boat whistle, alerting local citizens to gather at the wharf to assist the soldiers, some of whom were carried off on stretchers, while others, the walking wounded, limped ashore. Civilians loaded the men into wagons and drove them up Broad Street to the hospital, a mile away, with the town's church bells pealing in the background.

Beverly Hospital was staffed with qualified surgeons and nurses. While it was primarily a convalescent facility, a number of operations and amputations were apparently performed there as well. Local lore has amputated arms and legs packed in barrels for burial. Recovered patients returned to their units or were discharged, but the less fortunate were either buried near the hospital or claimed by their families for interment closer to home.

The prevailing middle-class social ethos at the outset of the war posited that it was "improper" for women to care for male hospital patients, while at the same time asserting that the "weaker sex" would not be equal to the physical demands of working in army hospitals. Needless to say, these premises were quickly discovered to be untrue and abandoned, and female nurses performed excellent work in hospitals across the North as well as with the armies. In large hospitals, under ideal conditions, each nurse theoretically had responsibility for ten patients and a cook was assigned for every thirty patients.

Unfortunately, ideal conditions did not always prevail. Georgeanna Woolsey, a nurse at Beverly, wrote that she and her sister Caroline:

Nurse Georgeana Woolsey (William E. Hughes)

have 100 men in our wards, all in bed. It is grimly amusing to hear the ward-surgeon say day after day, 'Milk and eggs for 38.' For two days there have been no eggs at all, and the milk rations are always short. The ladies are not allowed in the kitchen, or to have anything to do with the food for the patients. No steak and potatoes or milk punch come into this ward. We have opened a private account for bread, and milk, and butter and eggs, enough for this ward, with the village store. Our ward-surgeon has gone to a horse race, which seems a pretty long one! The surgeon-in-charge is kind in manner, and draws rations strictly according to army regulations; and seems to think that the stewards are the best persons to manage the food business. The object of the minor officers seems to be to subsist the men on nothing, and avoid making a row. We cannot keep our men alive; eleven of them have died in three days.

The Woolsey sisters, both experienced nurses, were dedicated to the individual welfare of their patients. The shortage of hospital rations led them to conclude that the cooks and stewards assigned to their wards: "make a clean steal of at least one meal a day from these two surgical wards - and the meals, when they are served from the hospital, are just the usual pork fat, and greasy slops."

Some hospital stewards and cooks were apparently poorly supervised, and stole and sold both food and medical supplies. The policy of not allowing nurses to assist in patient food preparation made it difficult for the sisters to cater to the soldiers' needs, but the Woolseys ended up spending their $12 monthly salaries and more on their "private account" to buy the food that their sickest patients required. They kept detailed descriptions of each soldier's needs in notebooks they carried in their apron pockets, and persisted in their efforts until they were allowed to personally see to it that meals were prepared in accordance with doctors' orders. Georgeanna also recorded the names and addresses of the dying so that their possessions could be sent to their families.

Many residents of Beverly and the surrounding communities were involved with the hospital, and townspeople collected extra food, clothing and money to help care for the patients. General Ulysses S. Grant's family was living in Burlington City in the last year of the war, and his daughter attended Saint Mary's Hall school in Burlington. On Christmas Day, local women and nurses prepared gift boxes and a special dinner for the hospitalized soldiers. Mrs. Grant helped prepare the meal and spent the day visiting the men, much to their delight.

Caroline Woolsey thought that at times the good intentions of some visitors went too far. On one occasion she wrote:

If I owned a hospital no philanthropist should ever enter. I could have pounded two benevolent old ladies yesterday on a tour of 'inspection' through my ward. One of my poor little boys, feverish and restless, tired of lying in bed for days and days, had crawled to the stove and been tucked

Nurse Caroline Woolsey, with her notepad and apron (William E. Hughes)

up in one of our rocking-chairs in his blanket. I had given him a hot drink and he had fallen into a doze, when these elderly philanthropists arrived, they shook him by the arm, yelling, 'Poor fellow, what's the matter, fever? Oh my! You're too near the stove; get right back to bed. There, now, that's it, you're too weak to sit up;' and so having saved one life as they thought, they passed on to the next.

On May 10, 1865, a month after the surrender of Confederate general Robert E. Lee, the War Department ordered the closing of a number of hospitals, including Beverly. When the hospital finally shut its doors on August 9, 1865, all remaining sick and wounded soldiers were transferred to White Hall Hospital across the Delaware River near Bristol, Pennsylvania. Despite good medical care for the times, a number of patients died at Beverly from either disease or as a result of combat wounds received in Virginia, including at Deep Bottom, Petersburg, Peeble's Farm, the Wilderness, Malvern Hill, Spotsylvania and Poplar Springs Church. Some soldiers arrived at the hospital dead of unknown causes.

A total of 6,332 men were admitted to Beverly Hospital during the year of its existence, for an average stay of thirty-two days. The largest number of soldiers present at one time was 1,818 on November 11, 1864. Hospital records indicate that 212 men died while patients at the hospital. Of this number, 147 were buried in a one-acre field donated for use as a cemetery by Joseph Weyman of Beverly. That impromptu burial ground, across the railroad tracks from the hospital, grew into Beverly National Cemetery. Although nothing remains of Beverly Hospital today, the national cemetery has expanded to hold the remains of about 47,000 men and women who have served their country. (Hughes, *Hospital at Beverly*; Austin, *Woolsey Sisters*)

Georgiana Willets
by
Sylvia Mogerman

Georgiana Willets (*Women's Work in the Civil War*)

Georgiana Willets of Jersey City was among a number of idealistic young women who hesitated to become nurses at the outset of the Civil War because of a Victorian misconception that their "delicacy or dignity" would be damaged by treating injured soldiers. When it became clear that this was not the case, Georgiana volunteered to go to the war.

She began her duties on May 13, 1864. Following the battle of the Wilderness she was assigned to the Second Army Corps' First Division hospital, established in a Catholic church in Fredericksburg, Virginia. Providing effective care for 150 badly injured men proved almost impossible for Willets and the one other nurse assigned to the hospital, but they did their best to keep the soldiers comfortable during a two-week tour of duty. After enduring the dreadful conditions at Fredericksburg, Willets assisted in the evacuation of 800 patients by ship down the Rappahannock River, and then left the vessel to help nurse 1,000 more wounded men lying on the ground and in wagons at Belle Plain before returning to Washington, D.C.

That summer Willets returned to the front on the supply steamer *Planter*. The armies had moved south, and she was assigned to the Second Corps' Second Division hospital at City Point, Virginia, where she managed several wards and the kitchen where food for the most seriously ill soldiers was prepared. Conditions there were not much better than Fredericksburg. Willets recalled that there were only "two basins with which to wash and dress wounds, almost no supplies and one small stove…." Despite all this, she remembered that the wounded considered her and the other nurses "Sunbeams," whose presence brought them some respite from the dreary horrors of the hospital.

Willets returned to Princeton, where she was brought up, in the fall of 1864, but went south again in early 1865, after volunteering for duty with the Tract Society of New York. The Society assigned her to Washington's Camp Barker, which offered shelter, medical services and educational opportunities for escaped slaves. Willets served as both teacher and nurse at the camp, recalling: "For the last 4 or 5 weeks of the existence of the Camp it was my practice every day and sometimes twice a day to visit the cabins to see if there were any sick; to attend to their necessities as far as I could do so…. The number of inmates was generally about 700….They generally arrived destitute of clothing, were chiefly women and children…." She became especially close to the women in the camp, and ministered to them and their children during a smallpox outbreak.

Georgiana Willets, an unsung and undeservedly long-forgotten New Jersey heroine of the Civil War, gave up a comfortable life to serve wounded soldiers and emancipated slaves. Little is known of her subsequent life.   (Moore, *Women of the War*; Berlin, *Wartime Genesis*)

"So Good, So Amiable and Pleasant"
Sarah Louisa Kellogg and the Port Royal Experiment
by
Robert F. MacAvoy

Freed slaves on the Sea Islands ready to work for wages.
(Library of Congress)

Sarah Louisa Kellogg was born March 9, 1828, at Elizabeth, New Jersey, to Elijah and Ann Marie Woodruff Kellogg. A school teacher by vocation, Kellogg was one of a number of zealous Northern white and African-American teachers who traveled to the Sea Islands off the coast of South Carolina to instruct ex-slaves liberated when the federal army and navy occupied the islands in 1861. These educators were members of "Gideon's Band," a group of idealists who labored to educate these newly free South Carolinians, who had previously been denied the opportunity by law.

The effort that Kellogg joined was part of the "Port Royal Experiment" (Port Royal being the Sea Islands' main harbor), a program initiated in 1861 in coastal South Carolina. In the "experiment," 10,000 former slaves successfully worked the plantations their former owners had fled, and were aided in their quest for self-sufficiency by a number of private charity organizations. By

Payday for freed slaves on the Sea Islands (*Harper's Weekly*)

selling their surplus cotton crops at a profit, the freedmen were able to acquire small property holdings of their own. In 1862, Union troops constructed Fort Mitchel, named for Union general Ormsby Mitchel, overseer of the Port Royal Experiment, who died of malaria on Hilton Head Island. The freed slaves subsequently founded their own town, with almost 1,500 residents, and named it Mitchelville in his honor. In 1865, following the assassination of President Lincoln, his successor, Tennessean Andrew Johnson, ended the successful Port Royal Experiment, which could have served as a pattern for progress, and returned the land to its previous white owners.

During Sarah Kellogg's time on Saint Helena, from 1862 to 1864, she shared a room with Charlotte Forten, a well-known young African-American teacher from Philadelphia. Unfortunately, Kellogg contracted tuberculosis and was forced to return to Elizabeth in January of 1865. Her friend and fellow teacher Arthur Summer lamented her departure, stating: "My dear friend, Miss Kellogg has gone away from us. She is ill; her lungs are sadly diseased, and so she has gone North. She was the light of the house, and the main pillar of the school. So good, so amiable, and pleasant, so efficient and sensible, so honest and kind – how can we get along in this gloomy house without her?"

Sarah Louisa Kellogg died of consumption in Elizabeth on June 24, 1866, having never married. On learning of her death, the Teacher's Committee of the American Freedmen's Union Commission reported: "The testimony of the Committee is unanimous in their estimate of the unselfishness of her devotion to the cause of the ignorant and the lowly. She can receive no greater crown of rejoicing than the thanks of those whom she has been the means of lifting into the light and privileges of a new and a free existence." Kellogg, who gave her life for her country as surely as any soldier, was buried in Hillside's Evergreen Cemetery with other members of her family. (*American Freedman*; Rose, *Rehearsal for Reconstruction*)

Sarah Louisa Kellogg's grave (Diane C. MacAvoy)

Lieutenant Oliver's Horse
by
Robert F. MacAvoy

In the summer of 1864, Private John Oliver of the 3rd New Jersey Volunteer Cavalry somehow acquired a spare horse, which he gave to his brother, First Lieutenant Charles Augustus Oliver of the 11th New Jersey Volunteer Infantry, whose regiment was camped nearby. Lieutenant Oliver was elated at the gift, which would save him from tramping alongside his fellow junior officers in the alternate dust and muck of Virginia's dirt roads. Although as a company grade officer Oliver was not authorized a horse, he apparently got away with riding rather than walking, at least for a time.

In early December, prior to the 11th's participation in a grand raid on the Weldon Railroad near Petersburg, Lieutenant Oliver was granted a leave of absence to return to New Brunswick, where his mother, Janet Oliver, was having a hard time coping with the death of her husband Francis, who had

Lieutenant Charles A. Oliver (John Kuhl)

been killed in action on December 13, 1862, at Fredericksburg, Virginia, while serving with the 28th New Jersey Volunteer Infantry. Prior to leaving for home, Oliver turned over the care of his prized equine possession to Private Charles Proctor, who served as cook for the 11th's officers.

Private Proctor, inexplicably nicknamed "Kate," was, in his position as cook, responsible for pots, pans, cooking utensils and rations, which he began to transport on Oliver's horse, more convenient than the supply train. Unfortunately, the regiment's officers began to pile their blankets and other personal baggage atop the horse as well, causing one wag to characterize the animal as an "animated furniture van." "Kate" Proctor protested, pointing out that the horse was overloaded, but was advised that if he couldn't manage the extra load, the officers would find another cook. Proctor, who knew he had a better deal cooking than fighting, dropped his objections.

On occasion the overloaded horse would stumble into a ditch and poor Proctor would have to unload him, drag him out and then repack everything. "Kate," employing much cursing and tugging, would always manage to get the horse into camp, but one morning when he went out to repack, he discovered, much to his surprise and grief, that the overburdened animal had died.

When Lieutenant Oliver returned to the regiment from leave, he was shocked to learn that his mount was dead, but neither his brother officers nor Private Proctor had the nerve to tell him the truth about the circumstances of its passing, and it was not until many years after the war that he learned the real cause of the animal's demise. (Marbaker, *History of the 11ᵗʰ New Jersey Volunteers*; MacAvoy family oral tradition)

The Colonel was a Lady
by
Joseph G. Bilby

The Kinsey family in 1864. left to right baby son J. B. Kinsey, J. Warner Kinsey, Emily Kinsey, cousin Margaret Kinsey (Margaret Buchholz/NGMMNJ)

John Warner Kinsey went to war in June 1864 as a first lieutenant and quartermaster of the 37th New Jersey Volunteer Infantry, a unit enlisted for 100 days of emergency service. No enlistment bounty was paid to these short-term soldiers, nor were they exempt from the draft, which made recruiting, to say the least, difficult. A newspaper account described the men of the 37th , who went off to war in late June, thusly: "There were many with one eye; several with less fingers than the regulations allowed; a few, long since past the age at which military service terminates; and scores of mere boys from fifteen years of age upwards."

Despite its less than perfect personnel, the 37th ended up at the front during the siege of Petersburg, initially detailed to unload supplies off steamers and serve with the ambulance corps and then into the trenches at the front under Confederate fire. While combat casualties were few, the regiment was ravaged by disease at Petersburg. First Lieutenant Parker Grubb, the 37th's adjutant and brother of regimental commander Colonel E. Burd Grubb, had marched off with the regiment on what he thought a great adventure with the words, "Remember to all at Sportsman's Hill and drink to friends gone far away with gusto." By August he was dead of typhoid fever. Lieutenant Grubb's friend Quartermaster Kinsey, who counted the day of his death "the saddest…during my entire life" and who later wrote movingly of Grubb that "his comrades loved him," survived.

Home once more, in February 1865 Kinsey reenlisted as quartermaster of the 40th New Jersey Volunteer Infantry. The 40th, the last regiment raised by New Jersey for the war, was assigned to the battle-hardened First New Jersey Brigade, then at Petersburg. The regiment participated in its first and last fight, the final great attack of the war, when Union forces overran the Petersburg defenses on April 2, 1865. The 40th marched in pursuit of General Lee's army, and then, the war over, north to Washington to participate in the victorious Union's Grand Review of the Armies.

On July 11, 1865, while the 40th New Jersey waited near Washington to be discharged from federal service, there was an unusual, unprecedented event in camp. Quartermaster Kinsey's wife, Emily Buzby Kinsey, was duly proclaimed a brevet or honorary lieutenant colonel by the regiment's Lieutenant Colonel J. Augustus Fay. Fay used a standard discharge form to declare Emily enlisted on June 4, 1865, and discharged on July 11, due to disability, and promoted the 24-year-old, 4'10" tall, dark-haired woman, whose civilian occupation was "quartermaster's wife," to brevet lieutenant colonel. Surgeon Charles E. Hall signed off on the brevet as a witness. Within days, the 40th was mustered out and Lieutenant Kinsey returned home to Crosswicks, with Emily's brevet promotion papers, unofficial, but impressive nonetheless.

Emily Kinsey's "brevet commission" (Margaret Buchholz/NGMMNJ)

In 1870, Mr. and Mrs. Kinsey opened in Barnegat City (now Barnegat Light) a seasonal "sportsmen's boarding hotel" known as "Kinsey's," which catered to fishermen and duck hunters. In the 1880s, Mr. Kinsey served as keeper of the Harvey Cedars Lifesaving Station. And, from all we know, the couple lived happily ever after, despite the disparity in rank. (Bilby & Goble, *Remember You Are Jerseymen*; Kinsey family papers, NGMMNJ; Buchholz, "The History of Harvey Cedars," bit.ly/HCHistory)

Jersey City Politics and the Great Hoboken
Bounty Jumper Sting of 1865
by
James M. Madden

As the Civil War dragged on, the demand for more men to fill the depleted ranks of the Union army escalated. At the outset of the conflict, many recruits enlisted out of patriotism, peer pressure, a lust for adventure or in search of a job, but by 1863 the hard hand of war had struck home across the North. With the willing already gone, escalating death tolls and the return home of the maimed, enthusiasm among remaining men of military age cooled considerably. The Confederacy had turned to conscription early in 1862, and by 1863 the Union followed suit. The Enrollment Act of 1863 established specific population-based troop quotas for states and towns, with a draft of military-age men to ensue if enough recruits were not secured to fill those requirements by a certain date. Federal provost marshals were assigned to each state, with deputies in each congressional district to supervise and enforce the effort.

The Enrollment Act required a conscripted man to serve himself, pay a $300 commutation fee for exemption from a particular draft, or pay a substitute to go in his place to free himself from the draft for the rest of the war. Commutation, much less the still higher cost of hiring a substitute, was impossible for the average laborer making less than $400 a year. Irish immigrants in particular came to view the war as "a rich man's war but a poor man's fight," and also feared that freed slaves would move north and compete with them for jobs at the low end of the pay scale. That anger led to three days of bloody rioting in New York City in July 1863 following the first draft. Relatively minor disturbances in Newark, New Jersey, at the same time led the federal government to temporarily suspend the draft in the state, and Governor Joel Parker promised to fill New Jersey's quota by voluntary enlistment.

To raise enough volunteers to meet quotas and escape a draft, cash bounties were offered to volunteers by federal, state, county and even city governments. Although moderate enlistment bounties had been offered to recruits in 1861 and 1862, by 1863 men could make between $500 and $1,000 in bounty money, with significant portions of those funds paid upfront in "hand money" on enlistment. Although Governor Parker encouraged counties and towns to offer generous bounties, and some new units were organized, the state failed to

The bait – announcement of the high bounties to be had in New Jersey (New York *Tribune*)

make its quota and New Jersey had its first draft in May 1864. The draft occasioned more merriment than dread, however, as large cities like Newark used taxpayer funds to buy commutation for their citizens and private "draft insurance" groups provided yet another way to legally escape service. By the time of the second draft in the fall of 1864, however, the federal government had abolished commutation, so a reluctant warrior was limited to but one way to escape service, hiring an increasingly expensive substitute, which municipalities failed to finance. Efforts to acquire high-bounty volunteers to head off a draft intensified.

The bounty system gave rise to a corrupt new world of entrepreneurship, with "bounty jumpers" and brokers making large amounts of fast money. Bounty jumpers would enlist in one town and be paid a bounty only to desert at the first opportunity and enlist in another municipality under another name. Brokers were professional schemers who managed traveling teams of professional jumpers offered to a town's recruiting agent to fill a draft quota.

The bounty-jumping business (and its allied entrepreneurial effort, substitute brokering) could reap enterprising scoundrels thousands of dollars a week. Towns just needed bodies credited to fill their quotas, which were tallied on enlistments, no matter what later happened with the recruit. In addition to jumpers, brokers and recruiters often secured men who were beyond draft age, drunk or physically disabled. Such scams required the collusion of not only the brokers and recruits themselves, but corrupt government officials, from local notary publics to examining physicians, draft rendezvous guards and even federal provost marshals. These situations were often exacerbated by local politicians running for reelection and mindful of their constituents' concerns about being drafted and the electoral benefit of attending to them. For such officials in the final years of the Civil War, dealing with bounty brokers, who could provide group quota-reducing enlistments, no matter their eventual outcome, had a certain appeal. Such was the case in Jersey City, New Jersey, in early 1865, when a statewide draft to take place in April, around the same time as municipal elections, was announced.

Jersey City Mayor Orestes Cleveland
(Library of Congress)

Jersey City's Democratic Mayor Orestes Cleveland positioned himself as the savior of voters in fear of the draft by announcing that he would raise money from local businessmen to pay large bounties, which would attract enough volunteer recruits to fill the city's quota. Jersey City's aldermen, also up for reelection, frantically tried to mitigate the effect of a potential draft on their individual wards by any means they could. One Democratic alderman talked federal officials into reassigning some recruits from another ward to his own, which elicited considerable protest from that ward's Republican alderman.

As Jersey City's politicians scrambled, across the Hudson United States Secret Service chief Colonel Lafayette Baker, considered a shady character himself by many, was zealously zeroing in on the bounty-jumping racket. With the assistance of Provost Marshal General James B. Fry, the colonel established headquarters at Manhattan's famed Astor House, and planned a major jumper sting in Hoboken, New Jersey. Hoboken was a docking point for Hudson River ferries, and a likely spot for jumpers operating in both New York and New Jersey. Baker employed army officers and enlisted men to impersonate recruiters, placed advertisements in local newspapers, and selected Hoboken's Odd Fellows Hall as center stage for the sting. To further avoid any suspicion, he also enlisted notorious New York bounty broker Theodore Allen, deputizing him to assist in the arrest of his associates and their jumper crews.

On the advice of Colonel Baker, Mayor Cleveland hired Allen, offering to pay him $126,000 (equivalent to some $3.4 million today) in bounty money to provide for recruits to fill the city's quota and bolster the mayor's reelection bid. Although Cleveland kept a campaign promise to put up the first $5,000 as an incentive himself, few wealthy citizens met his challenge and the goal of raising $126,000 by donation foundered badly. The desperate Cleveland then turned to borrowing the bounty money from the city's treasury and promoted the big payouts in local newspapers. The New York *Tribune* noted that "Mayor Cleveland sent a communication of increasing the bounties to relieve drafted men" to the paper.

Baker's bag of brokers and jumpers under guard (*Frank Leslie's Illustrated Newspaper*)

Although he was unaware of it, the advertising by Jersey City's mayor that major bounty money was available in New Jersey facilitated Colonel Baker's Hoboken sting. Jersey City's money would be paid out to the bounty jumpers the colonel and Allen lured across the Hudson. For several days in early March 1865, jumpers enlisted, received a portion of their bounty and were then allowed to walk out the back door of the Odd Fellows Hall while supposedly corrupt recruiting authorities looked the other way. These men, as Baker intended, took the ferry back to New York and spread the word that an "easy walk away" was available in Hoboken. Soon the ferries were transporting more passengers to New Jersey than business commuters to New York in the morning rush hour.

Nabbing the brokers and bounty jumpers. (Baker, *Authentic Stories*)

The trap was sprung on March 10, 1865. Recruiting was brisk early in the day, with an estimated 1,500 men gathering outside the Odd Fellows Hall. What the jumpers were unaware of was that guards were directing recruits to an upstairs hall rather than out the back door. In the early afternoon a broker became suspicious when none of his jumpers returned with money in hand. Glancing up at the Hall's second-story window, he spotted an armed guard and gave an alarm. The brokers scrambled for the ferry but most, identified by chalk marks scribed on the back of their jackets by one of Allen's men, were caught by Baker's detectives.

In the end, Baker rounded up 183 jumpers and 27 brokers. According to the *New York Times*, this collection of rogues was "the outscouring of the city slums, old prison birds, graduates from city institutions … and Tombs repeaters," as well as recognized bounty jumpers. A subsequent congressional investigation, however, revealed that 50 of those arrested were otherwise respectable men seeking a quick and easy buck. The arrested men were incarcerated at Fort Lafayette in New York Harbor to await trial. Colonel Baker was so proud of his haul that he requested permission from Fry to parade jumpers and brokers down Broadway in irons, "in order that the people may have a sight of them." Fry initially approved but later thought better of it and denied the request.

Four days after the sting, Cleveland met with Colonel Guido Ilges, a regular army officer in charge of the Hoboken recruiting effort, as well as with one of Allen's partners. Ilges maintained that he had to retain $300 of each bounty until the recruit reached his regiment, as insurance against desertion. Allen's man insisted that the cash in Ilges' hands was his as well as part of his fee for arranging the required number of recruits for Jersey City, arrested or not, and appealed directly to Provost Marshall General Fry in Washington for it by telegraph the following day. Fry, trying to sort out the mess, directed Colonel Ilges to refund the money "to the parties who advanced it."

Hoboken Odd Fellows Hall, site of the sting (Hoboken Free Public Library)

Misunderstanding the order, Ilges gave the money in his possession to Allen, rather than Mayor Cleveland, who had originally provided it. Allen thus effectively played both sides against the middle and ended up with almost all of the bounty money paid out to the jumpers. To make things worse, Fry subsequently telegraphed instructions to the New Jersey provost marshal to revoke any recruiting credits against the Jersey City quota since the credited men were in jail and not entering military service. Jersey City was out both money and recruit credits.

As word got out about the fiasco in some local papers, Cleveland's reelection prospects dimmed. The desperate mayor denied everything, claimed publicly that the draft quota had actually been exceeded, then quickly traveled to Washington to visit Fry in an effort to get his money back, or at least get credited for the ostensible recruits it had purchased. Fry finally ordered Baker to instruct Allen to return all of the Jersey City money to the mayor, who continued to assure the voters that there would be no draft as election day came closer. Rather than return the cash, however, Allen and his associates left the country, taking the money with them.

While the wrangling about credits and bounties continued, so did the waning days of the war. General Robert E Lee's army surrendered on April 9, 1865, and Jersey City held municipal elections two days later. Mayor Cleveland's Democratic "No Draft" ticket swept five of six wards, sweeping three Republican aldermen out of office. Cleveland won in a landslide, with 56% of the vote. With the war over, the draft was a thing of the past. There was no longer a market for recruits, and bounty jumpers were out of business. The mayor's clever election ploy, with more than a bit of luck, and the unplanned assistance of General Ulysses S. Grant, had worked.

Cleveland remained mayor, but Jersey City never regained its $126,000. After months of arguing with the War Department and several government investigations into what exactly had happened in Hoboken, the city had to settle for accepting draft quota credits for 168 men in the next draft during the next war. Unfortunately for Jersey City, the next war was the Spanish American War, in which there was no conscription. The next American draft was held during World War I, and, using the Civil War draft as an example not to be followed, quotas, commutation and bounties were all scrapped in an effort to create a more equitable system. Jersey City's credit, along with its money, was gone forever. (Baker *Spies, Traitors*; Bilby & Goble, *Jerseymen*; Fry, *Conklin and Blaine Fry*; Murdock, *Patriotism Limited*; *American Standard*; *Frank Leslie's Illustrated Newspaper*; *New York Times*; *New York Tribune*; Trenton *State Gazette*; Kinney, *Swindlers, Pimps and Vagabonds*)

The First Reunion
by
Joseph A. Truglio

New Jersey Civil War veterans engage in mock battle on the Kilpatrick farm, storming the hill and Hexamer's battery. (*Frank Leslie's Illustrated Newspaper*)

At 3 P.M. on Thursday, August 29, 1878, the still air of rural Sussex County, New Jersey, was shattered by booming cannon fire, signaling the start of what was intended as a great mock battle staged by New Jersey veterans to commemorate their Civil War service. The event was the culmination of a three-day gathering of many of the state's Union army veterans held on the farm of New Jersey native son Major General Hugh Judson Kilpatrick.

The event was conceived and organized by "Kill-Cavalry" Kilpatrick with the intent of kick-starting his short-circuited political career. As minister to Chile in the late 1860s, the former general ran afoul of the Grant administration and other Republican party officials, which cost him his appointment. Recalled in 1870, Kilpatrick returned to the United States and took to the lecture circuit, damning

Author Joe Truglio stands by the historic marker indicating the site of Kilpatrick's grand reunion. (Bob Gerber)

President Grant as a drunk, among other things, and settled into a role as a "gentleman farmer" in Deckertown between tours. His agricultural efforts were quite successful and in the early 1870s he joined the local chapter of the Patrons of Husbandry, commonly known as The Grange.

Veterans march past the Kilpatrick home. (*Frank Leslie's Illustrated Newspaper*)

Always ambitious, Kilpatrick longed for a return to the political life, and hit upon the idea of sponsoring a grand reunion and celebration of New Jersey war veterans, ostensibly intended to honor the former soldiers' service but also as a way of promoting his potential candidacy for a seat in Congress. The gathering would be highlighted by a battle reenactment before what the general hoped would be a host of happy spectators and voters.

Kilpatrick, as was his wont, thought in grand terms when planning the event. He contacted various veteran organizations to invite their members and advertised in local papers as well as the larger New York press, announcing to the public that such notables as President Rutherford B. Hayes, former Army of the Potomac commander and New Jersey Governor George B. McClellan, Generals Philip Sheridan and William T. Sherman, would be among the attendees. Kilpatrick contracted with various New York City vendors to supply food and drink to those who attended, reserving a cut of the profits for himself. Although he boasted of having an aqueduct system that would supply water to the crowds, it failed, coincidentally providing a market for the 10,000 barrels of beer his vendors made available to quench the thirst of participants and spectators. A large area at the base of a ridge in front of the Kilpatrick home was cleared as a "battlefield," and the veterans of Hexamer's old Battery A, 1st New Jersey Artillery, were invited to man artillery pieces atop a knoll at the focal point of the proposed "attack." One gun was positioned at the train station to signal the arrival of each train carrying veterans and spectators to the event.

A group of local citizens assisted Kilpatrick in organizing the reunion despite regional press warnings of the hazards that would befall the little village of Deckertown and its population of 600 souls. Editorials warned of "pick-pockets in the streets and the resorts being filled with base women." The townsfolk prepared. Unafraid, and perhaps with an eye on profit, they decorated the streets and homes with banners welcoming the arrival of visitors.

And arrive they did. Veterans, spectators and New York City street people stormed the area. Five trains a day carrying 400 passengers each rolled into Deckertown. Still more people walked, rode in wagons, on horses, and marched together as individuals and in groups. Strolling musicians entertained, and the masses munched peanuts, drank beer, and engaged in games of chance in the biggest carnival Sussex County had ever witnessed. Estimates of 4,000 veterans and 40,000 spectators on hand did not seem out of place. On Monday evening, August 26, Kilpatrick staged a performance of his play "Allatoona", with the general in the wings prompting the actors. The evening's entertainment ended with a serenade honoring Mrs. Kilpatrick, followed by a spectacular fireworks display.

Camp at Deckertown (*Frank Leslie's Illustrated Newspaper*)

Festivities resumed in late afternoon the following day, as Kilpatrick led the veterans on horseback in a march from town to the site of the "battle." A large tent and grandstand had been erected in the field to accommodate visiting dignitaries. Kilpatrick then led off in a round of speech making. The absence of officials the general had advertised as honored guests was conspicuous. There was no Hayes, nor McClellan, Sherman or Sheridan. To take up the slack, General John Robinson, head of the Grand Army of the Republic and the ever popular general, politician and scamp Daniel Sickles were there to "rally the troops." That night a banquet was held in the tent for veterans and dignitaries.

Wednesday was a day of rehearsal for the 4,000 "combatants" and the reenactment took place on Thursday, August 29. Troops lined up and made several charges up the ridge to capture the guns. Cannons boomed and rifles fired. Kilpatrick, riding his speckled white horse and waving a flag, rode up and down the line whooping and hollering. It was a grand event and all the participants, particularly the general, seemed to enjoy themselves. The crowd loved it. And then everyone went home.

In the aftermath, the Kilpatrick farm looked as if a real battle had taken place there. Crops had been cut down before they ripened and about seventy acres were trampled into dust by the visitors and guests, and most of the field-dividing fences had been torn down. No one needed to worry about the general's finances, however, since his percentage from the merchants and vendors more than compensated for his losses.

General Kilpatrick addresses the veterans. (*Frank Leslie's Illustrated Newspaper*)

In the long run, the massive effort did not have the anticipated effect on Kilpatrick's political ambitions. He failed in his attempt to gain a seat in Congress in 1880. However, he had been active in the movement to prevent Grant from running for a third term, and had campaigned vigorously for Chester A. Arthur as a vice presidential candidate. Kilpatrick was eventually rewarded for these efforts with reappointment as minister to Chile. He left for Santiago in June of 1881, although for but a short term. The general was suffering from Bright's disease, a kidney ailment that would today be characterized as chronic nephritis, and which some attributed to his years of campaigning in the saddle. By mid-September, he was confined to his bed, and at 9:45 P.M. on December 2, 1881, Hugh Judson Kilpatrick died, at the age of 45. He lay in state at his home and was then buried in the Valdivieso family vaults at the Catholic Church of Sagrario in Santiago, at Chilean government expense. A year later his body was returned to the United States and reinterred in the West Point cemetery, with a monument over his grave paid for by his classmates and former troopers.

Today, little remains to remind us of Kilpatrick's reunion. The "battlefield" is a lush meadow, the stately Kilpatrick residence is gone, and its site surrounded by modern homes. Only a signpost on a nearby country lane announces what happened there so long ago. But the general's event stands, 132 years afterward, as the first Civil War battle reenactment in New Jersey, and, despite the personal motives of its creator, the first large-scale commemoration of the service of the state's Civil War veterans. (Martin, *Kill-Cavalry*; *New York Times*)

The Battle of Princeton Junction
by
John W. Kuhl

A frequent question from audiences of all ages for those who make presentations on New Jersey's role in the Civil War is whether there were any battles within the borders of the state. While there were considerable and sometimes bitter internal discussions on the war in New Jersey politics, there were no actual battles fought in New Jersey during the war. There was, however, a notable postwar fight in the state that, while not as large as Judson Kilpatrick's 1878 mock battle at Deckertown, proved a much bloodier affair.

A number of veterans' organizations were formed in the years after the last shot of the Civil War echoed into history, as former soldiers returned to a tamer and more humdrum civilian life. Veterans joined these associations for social and personal reasons, but also to lobby for veteran pension benefits. Chief among these groups was the Grand Army of the Republic, usually referred to as the GAR, founded in 1866. The GAR grew slowly at first, but began

A panorama of the Princeton Junction GAR encampment
(*Frank Leslie's Illustrated Newspaper*)

to expand rapidly during the early 1880s, with local chapters formed across the North in most sizeable towns. The New Jersey GAR's Fourth Annual Encampment was scheduled for the week beginning Monday, September 3, 1883, for an open area at Princeton Junction just east of the college town, a site that was convenient for veterans traveling by rail from distant parts of the state. The temporary camp was named Camp Olden in honor of Charles Olden, the New Jersey governor at the outset of the Civil War, who also gave his name to a camp outside of Trenton where a number of regiments were organized in 1861.

Individuals and groups of veterans continued to arrive at Princeton Junction through midweek, bringing the number of GAR members at the camp to around a thousand men. Also arriving as invited guests were the 4th and 6th Regiments of the New Jersey National Guard. Meetings, speeches, drills, reviews, and inspections were a daily occurrence through Wednesday, when a sham battle between the veterans and Guardsmen was planned, to be followed the next day by a culminating "Grand Review" of both parties.

The veterans had arrived in camp determined to enjoy themselves. The isolation of their camp may have limited some pursuits of the flesh but the diversion of alcohol was close to hand. Disregarding the societal effects of strong drink, a controversial aspect of nineteenth-century life that eventually led to a failed attempt at national prohibition, had previously been a subject of criticism directed at the GAR. The Lambertville *Record* editorialized that the first state encampment in 1880 had been a "success, if crowds and the large sale of beer are indications—But we very much question whether any good comes from these affairs, and we know that a great deal of evil results." Some Democratic politicians, foes of the Republican-leaning veterans, had earlier charged that "two-thirds of its survivors had come out of the war with intemperance fixed upon them." To these folks, the GAR was the "Grand Army of Drunkards." Temporarily freed from strictures of civilian domesticity and

Louis R. Schoenheit in a postwar picture as GAR post commander (Hunterdon County Historical Society)

employment, some of the boys at Princeton Junction seem to have set out to prove the critics' case. A *Frank Leslie's Illustrated Newspaper* staff artist recording the encampment sketched a provost marshal hauling an apparently inebriated offender off with a firm grip on the scruff of his neck while another man slouched on the ground obviously hung over from "too much camp."

From a spectator's view, the highlight of the week was the mock skirmish on Wednesday. Between four and five thousand people gathered in pleasant weather to witness the "battle." At 4:30 in the afternoon, about 250 GAR men armed with rifles and five cannon were stationed in the open field to represent the Union. Some 250 similarly armed men of the National Guard who represented the "Rebels" mustered in the camp area. As the *Trenton Times* reported:

"The battle was begun by the Rebel skirmishers, who rushed forward to the advancing Union forces. There was lively skirmishing on both sides, and the skirmish lines were finally driven in. The two armies advanced in line of battle and each side alternately drove the other. The militia maneuvered excellently, but the Grand Army men were more used to real fight than to sham, and in the excitement of the contest they broke away from all restraint, and the opposing sides rushed so closely together that the guns were discharged directly into the faces of the men. Muskets were even clubbed, and two staff officers belabored each other with canes. All this was good-humored, though very reckless, as was seen a moment later, when a momentary drawing back of the lines showed men lying thickly on the ground where the fight had been the hottest. Colonel [William H.] Cooper [of the 6th New Jersey National Guard] instantly brought the battle to an end by surrendering the Rebel forces, and the soldiers turned their attention to their injured comrades. Many of them had received only slight burns and scratches, and walked off without needing any attention, but thirteen were so badly hurt that they had to call upon surgeon [Edmund L. B.] Godfrey of the Sixth Regiment."

Among the thirteen serious wounds were those described as "hurt leg, gun wad in leg, face lacerated and painfully burned, shot in the left breast, arm hurt." The *Times* went on to say:

"All but two or three of these were able to be around the camp after their wounds had been dressed. Many of the injuries are very painful but none are dangerous. The injuries were all inflicted by wadding from the guns. Surgeon Godfrey explicitly denies the reports that any of the wounds were from ramrods or pistol balls, as was stated by some of the morning newspapers."

Augustus Blanchett during the Civil War (John Kuhl)

Three veterans had to be sent home for additional medical care. Augustus Blanchet, a former major in the 27th New Jersey Volunteer Infantry, of Torbert GAR Post No. 24 in Morristown, had the muscles of his right arm shot through. Blanchet had resigned his commission for disability in April 1863, but had apparently recovered enough over the years to charge into the fight with the New Jersey National Guard. Albert Harrison, once a sergeant in the 14th New Jersey Volunteer Infantry and a member of Arrowsmith GAR Post No. 61 in Red Bank, had been twice wounded in the war. Harrison was hit in the left thigh by a buckshot at Cold Harbor and had a finger shot off his right hand at Petersburg.

His new wound was more serious than his wartime injuries and was alleged to have been caused by a fired ramrod, despite Surgeon Godfrey's claim to the contrary. Indeed, one rifle was turned in with its ramrod missing. Interestingly enough, Harrison would claim his 1883 wound in his subsequent application for a Civil War veteran's pension. The third serious casualty was German immigrant Louis Richard Schoenheit of Morris County's German Valley (renamed Long Valley in the anti-German hysteria of World War I). Schoenheit, onetime commander of his local GAR post, had served as a private in

Albert Harrison during the Civil War (John Kuhl)

the 5th New Jersey Volunteer Infantry. Wounded in the leg at the battle of Second Bull Run, he had recuperated and then joined the 2nd New Jersey Volunteer Cavalry. For these three men, the Fourth Annual Encampment at Princeton Junction, like their war, was over.

The Grand Review came off as scheduled on Thursday but did not achieve the expectations of its organizers. To the disappointment of many, one-legged New York General Dan Sickles, a ubiquitous presence at such affairs, who was scheduled to review the troops, never showed up, and only a handful of spectators came to watch. The entire contingent of National Guardsmen turned out for the parade and marched admirably but only three or four GAR posts joined the line of march. The *Trenton Times* reporter noted that the GAR men "didn't see the use of marching around in the dust for nothing." No doubt they had been there and done that in the 1860s enough times to last them the rest of their lives. Although local newspapers continued to report on the casualties for several days, the camp broke up by the weekend and all the participants went home, a bit battered and hung over, no doubt, but apparently satisfied.

Annual state encampments, minus the hand-to-hand combat, would continue up to the eve of World War II, when the last of the old veterans had passed or were homebound and the GAR was no more. Though mostly forgotten now, the Fourth New Jersey State Encampment, with its battle of Princeton Junction, could certainly be one of the wildest and most remarkable of these events.

(*Trenton Times*; *Frank Leslie's Illustrated Newspaper*; *Hunterdon County Democrat*; *Hunterdon Republican*; NARA pension records; *NJAG Report for 1883*; McConnell, *Glorious Contentment*)

Addendum

The Battle of Princeton Junction was not the first mock battle to turn bloody, nor the last. On March 8, 1861, on the eve of the Civil War, the Lambertville (N.J.) *Beacon* reported a similar incident in Easton, Pennsylvania, across the Delaware River from Phillipsburg, New Jersey. Two militia units engaged two others atop a hill outside Easton and their enthusiasm carried them beyond the efforts of officers to restrain them. There were several broken swords and twelve to fifteen bayonet wounds to arms, ears, hands and faces before the combatants could be separated. In more modern times, the 15th New Jersey Infantry of the North-South Skirmish Association, designated the official New Jersey honor guard during the Civil War Centennial, participated in a reenactment of the battle of Antietam on the original battlefield in September of 1962. They were attacked by Confederate reenactors near "Bloody Lane" and the author of this essay was assaulted by an overenthusiastic Rebel swinging the butt of his musket at head height, an experience that prompted him to end his reenacting career. (Lambertville *Beacon*) - John Kuhl

Reverend Robinson and the Meaning of the War
by
Joseph G. Bilby

In the aftermath of the Civil War, New Jersey's black veterans formed their own Grand Army of the Republic (GAR) veterans' association posts, beginning around 1880. These posts included Major General David Hunter Post No. 105 in Princeton, Major General William Birney Post No. 95 in Red Bank, Colonel Robert Gould Shaw Post No. 27 and Isaac M. Tucker Post No. 65 in Newark, William P. Robeson Post No. 51 in Camden, Major Martin Delany Post No. 53 in Atlantic City, Thomas Hamilton Post No. 56 in Trenton, Clinton B. Fisk Post No. 114 in Atlantic Highlands and Captain Andrew Cailloux Post No. 119 in Asbury Park. The latter post was named after one of a small number of black officers in the Union army, who was killed in action while heroically leading a charge at Port Hudson, Louisiana, in 1863.

Although there was no official national policy to segregate GAR posts, the organization came to reflect the racial realities of the nation as a whole. Some posts, however, were integrated to a greater or lesser degree, and some United States Colored Troops veterans may also have been members of predominantly white New Jersey posts. The GAR purchased burial plots for its members in various cemeteries around the state, and interments were completely integrated, with white veterans occasionally providing military honors for their black comrades.

There were almost certainly Civil War veterans from the Cailloux Post in the audience on June 17, 1887, when Reverend James Francis Robinson of the Methodist Episcopal Zion Church in Asbury Park vigorously answered the assertion of the town's founder, James Bradley, that beach and boardwalk segregation were justified since equal rights in America were "an impossibility." In a fiery sermon with political overtones, Robinson not only pointed out that the resort town of Asbury Park would fail to function without its black workers but that the country as a whole owed African-Americans a debt of gratitude. "We helped save the Union," exclaimed Robinson.

In his military allusion, Robinson, who may have been a veteran himself, might have been making a veiled reference to Bradley, who, thirty-one years old at the outbreak of the war, not only failed to serve, but also made a fortune selling brushes to the military. "We are a free people," said Robinson, "and we have the same rights by law as our fellow citizens whose skins are white." In a subsequent speech in New York, he ventured the opinion that reading Bradley's *Asbury Park Journal* made a reader think "it was edited in Georgia." (McConnell, *Glorious Contentment*; Wolff, *Asbury Park*; *New York Times*. Adapted from Bilby and Ziegler, *Asbury Park*)

Fort Sumter Yes, Baseball No?
by
Thomas R. Burke

Abner Doubleday was born June 26, 1819, at Ballston Spa, New York. His father, Ulysses, was a veteran of the War of 1812 who served two terms in the U.S. Congress in the 1830s.

Doubleday attended school in Auburn and Cooperstown, New York, and in 1838 was appointed to the United States Military Academy at West Point. He graduated in 1842, along with future generals James Longstreet, William Rosecrans and D.H. Hill, after which he served as an artillery officer in the Mexican War and fought the Seminole Indians in Florida.

Abner Doubleday during the war. (National Archives)

In 1858, Captain Doubleday was assigned to Charleston, South Carolina, as second in command of the harbor's defenses under Major Robert Anderson. On April 12, 1861, at Fort Sumter, he aimed the cannon that fired the first Union shot of the Civil War. Promotions came quickly to Doubleday as the war progressed, and by early 1862 he was a brigadier general. Doubleday fought at the Second Battle of Bull Run, Antietam, Fredericksburg and Gettysburg, where he commanded the entire Union force on the battlefield for a brief period on July 1, before being relieved of command. Slightly wounded the following day, he spent the remainder of the war primarily behind a desk, overseeing court-martial proceedings. In November 1863, Doubleday traveled with President Lincoln to Gettysburg for the dedication of the national cemetery. He and his wife Mary also attended many social affairs with the Lincolns in Washington.

While stationed in San Francisco after the war, Doubleday was granted a franchise on the first street-cable-car system, which is still running there today. In 1873, he retired from the army and subsequently moved to Mendham, New Jersey, where he spent the rest of his life. While in Mendham, he became a member and later president of the newly established Theosophical Society, a cult-like philosophical/religious organization, and was also active in veterans' reunions and in organizing the management of Gettysburg National Park.

Doubleday spent much of his Mendham years writing and produced two significant works on the Civil War, *Reminiscences of Forts Sumter and Moultrie* in 1876, and *Chancellorsville and Gettysburg* in 1882. General Doubleday passed away from heart disease on January 26, 1893, in Mendham, and was interred at Arlington National Cemetery.

Despite his accomplishments, Mendham's Abner Doubleday became more famous for something he had nothing to do with. In 1908, some fifteen years after his death, the Mills Commission — a group empanelled by then New Jersey resident, former star pitcher, baseball executive and sporting goods dealer Albert G. Spalding to "research" the origins of baseball — cited Abner Doubleday as the inventor of the game in central New York. Doubleday had never claimed any such thing during his lifetime, and there was no reliable evidence for any connection, but Spalding was determined to prove that baseball was a totally American game, with no connection to similar British sports. The myth was perpetuated by the Baseball Hall of Fame in Cooperstown, New York, in its earliest years, but most considered the story thoroughly debunked in the latter part of the 20th century. Nevertheless, the legend persists. In late 2010, Bud Selig, the Commissioner of Baseball, wrote in a letter regarding the general's place in sports history, "I really believe that Abner Doubleday is the 'Father of Baseball.'" (*New York Times*; Barthel, *Abner Doubleday*)

A Southern Sailor's Story
by
Robert F. MacAvoy

The naval duel between the USS *Monitor* and the CSS *Virginia* (formerly the USS *Merrimack*) took place on March 8-9, 1862, at Hampton Roads, Virginia. For the first time in naval history, two ironclad warships engaged each other, fighting to a draw. The contest itself is a well-known incident of Civil War history. It is safe to say, however, that the fact that the last surviving sailors from both ships ended up in New Jersey is a little known aspect of the state's Civil War story.

John McGuire served as a fireman or "stoker" aboard the *Virginia*. In June 1914, McGuire, then a retired New Jersey railroad worker, was notified by unnamed officials in Washington, D.C., that he was the last surviving sailor of the crew of the *Virginia*. (McGuire was erroneously listed as "McQuinn" on *Virginia*'s roster.) That determination was contested the following month by Andrew G. Peterson, a Finnish soldier of fortune who enlisted in the Confederate navy in 1862 and was then living in Grass Valley, California. Peterson was a noncommissioned officer on the *Virginia*'s crew who remembered McGuire as a stoker on the vessel. Peterson died five months later, however, leaving McGuire as the undisputed survivor of the *Virginia*'s naval crew. (The crew also included a number of detached-service army artillerymen, perhaps the last of whom, William Francis Drake, was still alive in 1928 in the Confederate Soldiers Home in Raleigh, North Carolina.)

McGuire, who was born in Ireland, emigrated to the United States as a young man in 1857. He was living in the South at the beginning of the Civil War and enlisted in the Confederate navy. After the war he moved to Elizabeth, New Jersey, where he worked on the Elizabeth and Somerville Railroad ferryboat, *Red Jacket*, which ran between Elizabeth and New York. He relocated to Somerset County around 1871, living first as a boarder in Bridgewater and later moving to a boardinghouse owned by Katherine Gilmore in Somerville, where he spent the rest of his life. He was then employed by the Jersey Central Railroad, spending the last twenty years of his career as a brakeman. McGuire retired on a $21.50 monthly pension around 1906, and spent the remaining ten years of his life close to friends, the railroad, and his garden. McGuire never married and was always reticent about his

John McGuire's grave marker (Diane C. MacAvoy)

wartime experience on the *Virginia*, fearing that his New Jersey neighbors would "fail to appreciate any heroism on his part in the conflict between the North and the South."

McGuire died on March 13, 1916, in the Gilmore home on Division Street in Somerville, after a short bout with what was described as gastritis, and was buried in the Immaculate Conception Catholic Cemetery on Union Avenue in Somerville. In an interesting case of historical coincidence, the last naval crewman of the USS *Monitor*, the CSS *Virginia*'s antagonist, is also buried in New Jersey soil. Andrew J. Fenton, a U.S. Navy veteran, died on April 18, 1945, and is interred in Overlook Cemetery in Bridgeton, Cumberland County. (Somerset (NJ) *Democrat*; New Brunswick (NJ) *Times*; *New York Times*; *Washington Post*. Research assistance provided by Stuart Otts and Steven Glazer.)

From Newton to the Washita
by
Robert Gerber

Robert M. West was born in Newton, New Jersey, on September 16, 1834. West joined the United States Mounted Rifles as a private on April 12, 1856, and served until he was discharged on February 5, 1861. With the outbreak of the Civil War, West, like many Jerseymen, crossed the border to Pennsylvania to enlist and was commissioned captain of Battery G, 1st Pennsylvania Light Artillery. He was subsequently promoted to the rank of major and then colonel in the 1st Artillery. What his actual command was is unclear, as the regiment's various batteries served in different locations. In 1864, Colonel West was transferred to the 5th Pennsylvania Cavalry and assumed command of that regiment. The 5th was involved in a number of raids and fights during the siege of Petersburg in the last year of the war.

Robert M. West (Robert Gerber)

On April 1, 1865, West was brevetted brigadier general of volunteers for gallantry and meritorious conduct at the battle of Five Forks, Virginia.

Honorably mustered out of service on August 7, 1865, West applied for a commission in the regular army and was appointed a captain in the U. S. 7th Cavalry on July 28, 1866. The 7th's nominal commander was Colonel Andrew Jackson Smith but its field commander was Lieutenant Colonel George Armstrong Custer. Like a number of other officers in the 7th, West had serious disagreements with Custer, most notably following the June 1868 shooting of two of his men for desertion. When Custer was court-martialed at Fort Leavenworth on September 15, 1867, for leaving his command without authorization to visit his wife, the deserter-shooting issue was also brought before the court. Although Custer was suspended from duty for a year for his conduct, West brought a charge of murder against his commander in civil court. Following a few days of testimony, however, the judge dismissed the case due to insufficient evidence.

In retaliation, Custer brought charges of "drunkenness on duty" against Captain West. Although his fellow officers testified that West was indeed a heavy and sometimes uncontrollable drinker, they agreed he was still one of the best company commanders in the regiment. Convicted on some of his commander's charges, Captain West was sentenced to a suspension from duty and forfeiture of pay for two months.

When Custer returned from his own suspension in October 1868, he still harbored resentment towards West and refused to shake his hand. On the morning of November 27, 1868, the 7th Cavalry, under George Armstrong Custer, attacked Chief Black Kettle's Southern Cheyenne and Arapaho village along the Washita River in present-day Oklahoma. Captain West was in the thick of the action, leading a two-company battalion of the 7th in the attack.

Realizing that he no longer had Custer's sympathy and possibly cognizant that his drinking was interfering with his duties, West resigned his commission on March 1, 1869. General Philip Sheridan promised him the sutlership at the new Fort Sill in Indian Territory, but before he could open for business, Robert West died, a long way from Newton, near Fort Arbuckle on September 3, 1869. (Carroll, *The Custer Autograph Album*; Frost, *George Armstrong Custer Legends*; Hatch, *The George Armstrong Custer Companion*)

Elias Wright – Atlantic City Pioneer
by
Thomas R. Burke

Elias Wright. (USAMHI)

Elias Wright was born on June 22, 1830, in Durham, New York. He moved to Atlantic County, New Jersey, in 1852, when Jonathan Pitney and Samuel Richards were pushing a railroad across the Pinelands to Absecon Island, where Atlantic City was created two years later. A schoolteacher in New York, Wright, sensing opportunity in the new city by the sea, took up surveying, an occupation in much demand.

With the outbreak of the Civil War, Wright helped organize a company of volunteers that became part of the 4th New Jersey Volunteer Infantry. He was commissioned a second lieutenant in the 4th's Company G on August 17, 1861, and promoted to first lieutenant of Company D in January 1862. Lieutenant Wright, along with most of the 4th New Jersey, was captured at the battle of Gaines Mill when the regiment was overrun, and confined at Richmond's Libby Prison. Exchanged in August, Wright and the 4th fought again at Second Bull Run and Crampton's Gap, were he was wounded. When Captain Charles Meyer of Company A resigned his commission, Wright was promoted to captain and commander of the company, which he led at Fredericksburg and Salem Church. Wright resigned from his position with the 4th on June 23, 1863, to accept appointment as major of a new African-American regiment, the 1st United States Colored Infantry.

Wright was promoted to lieutenant colonel of the 1st and then colonel of the 10th United States Colored Infantry. With the organization of the Twenty-fifth Army Corps, the largest African-American unit in United States army history, in December of 1864, Wright was elevated to brigade command and in January 1865 received the brevet (honorary) rank of brigadier general, in recognition of his war service. With the end of the war, Wright resigned his commission to return to civilian life on June 17, 1865.

Wright returned to Atlantic City to resume his career as a surveyor and civil engineer. He became an authority on land titles and managed properties in the vicinity of Weymouth until 1873, when he was hired by industrialist and iron-and-steel lobbyist Joseph Wharton, who was buying up as much of the Pinelands as he could in order to corner the market on a potential source of drinking water for

Philadelphia. Wright's job entailed surveying and searching the titles on the 150 square miles of land Wharton bought in the Pines. Many of these titles were complex and some went back as far as 1720. The project took twenty-eight years to complete and filled three volumes with one of the most complete records of its kind in the United States at that time. Elias Wright died on January 2, 1901, and was buried in Greenwood Cemetery in Pleasantville, New Jersey. Wharton's plan failed when the state legislature prohibited water sales out of state, and the "Wharton Tract" that Wright surveyed was eventually sold to New Jersey as a state forest in 1954. (Bilby and Goble, *Remember You Are Jerseymen*; Hall, *Daily Union History of Atlantic City and County*; Johnson, *Boardwalk Empire*; Lurie & Mappen, *Encyclopedia of New Jersey*; bit.ly/EliasWright; bit.ly/EWrightGrave)

Elias Wright grave marker in Pleasantville (Russ Dodge)

A Confederate Cemetery in New Jersey:
Finn's Point, Fort Delaware and Fort Mott
by
Dr. David G. Martin

The history of Finn's Point National Cemetery in New Jersey is intimately connected with the story of nearby Forts Delaware and Mott. Construction of a fort on Pea Patch Island in the Delaware River, within sight of Finn's Point, began in 1817. Its purpose was to defend the lower Delaware against a possible enemy incursion upriver to Philadelphia, since the vulnerability of America's coastal cities became all too obvious through the British attacks on Baltimore, Washington and New Orleans during the War of 1812. Progress on the fort's construction proceeded so slowly and sporadically, however, that it became obsolete before completion and was demolished in 1833. A new fort of brick and masonry was constructed between 1848 and 1859. On completion, Fort Delaware was the largest fort in the country at that time.

The fort was never attacked during the Civil War but was soon put to another use. It was quickly impressed into service as a prison for court-martial-convicted Union soldiers and Southern sympathizers. Its greatest use, however, was to hold captured Confederate soldiers. A huge influx of prisoners came to Fort Delaware in July 1863 when most of the Confederate soldiers captured at Gettysburg were sent there. By the end of that summer there were some 11,000 prisoners on the island, and by the end of the war it had housed over 33,000 captives.

Confederate Memorial at Finn's Point National Cemetery (David Martin)

Wooden barracks were erected for the common soldiers and many of the officers were quartered in the fort itself. Ten Confederate generals were imprisoned at Fort Delaware at one time or another, including J.J. Pettigrew, James J. Archer, Jeff Thompson, Ed Johnson, George "Maryland" Steuart and Joseph Wheeler. Due to crowding, disease, and a poor supply of drinking water, over 2400 prisoners (and a number of Union guards, as well) died on the island. This mortality rate, though, was not nearly as high as at some of the other major prison camps of the war, such as Elmira in New York and Andersonville in Georgia, both of which had a death rate of over 25%.

The high number of deaths occurring at Fort Delaware soon required more burial space than was available on the swampy ground of Pea Patch Island. Bodies needed to be transported off the island to one of the nearby shores, and New Jersey was chosen. The plot of land selected for the fort's cemetery was on Finn's Point, where the federal government owned property it had bought to erect a battery to guard the river. The location was converted to a cemetery by 1863 and eventually 2,436 Confederate soldiers who died at Fort Delaware prison were buried there, along with 135 Union soldiers who died while serving as guards at the fort.

Union Memorial at Finn's Point National Cemetery (David Martin)

The site was declared a national cemetery on October 3, 1875, at the request of former Confederate General James L. Kemper, who was then serving as governor of Virginia and was not happy with the poor maintenance of the site. Soon afterwards, the bodies of 187 Confederate prisoners and the Union guards who had been buried on Pea Patch Island near Fort Delaware were reinterred in the new cemetery. A Union monument was erected in 1879 in honor of the guards who died at Fort Delaware prison and a Confederate monument was erected in 1910 by, surprisingly, the federal government. The Confederate monument is an 85-feet-tall concrete obelisk faced with granite. It lists the name and regiment of each soldier buried in the cemetery, though individual graves cannot be identified. Each of the seven Confederate burial trenches has at its end an iron plate with a quatrain from Theodore O'Hara's poem "Bivouac of the Dead." These plates were installed by the federal government around 1885. The identities of Union soldiers buried in individual gravesites in the cemetery were once known but the records were lost over the years. The names of 105 of those men are inscribed on the Union monument, however. In 1936, the Union monument was moved a few feet and a Greek-style cupola was placed over it.

Sadly, there are no identified individual Civil War soldier graves of either side in the cemetery. The mortal remains of all soldiers, blue or gray, buried there rest in anonymity, except for their names carved on the stone monuments.

Soldiers continued to be buried in the cemetery from the Spanish American War through World War I, and thirteen white-marble headstones mark the graves of German soldiers who died while prisoners at nearby Fort Dix during World War II. Finn's Point National Cemetery had 3033 burials as of the end of the year 2008. It is now closed for new interments with the exception of cremated remains.

Finn's Point was placed on the National Register of Historic Places in 1978. The site contains 115 acres and is surrounded by Killcohook National Wildlife Refuge and adjacent to Fort Mott State Park. The name "Finn's Point" probably comes from Finnish settlers who lived in New Sweden in the early 1600s before the area came under Dutch, then English control.

The predecessor of nearby Fort Mott was built between 1872 and 1876 to help guard the Delaware River approaches to Philadelphia. The current fort was begun in 1897, and was named in honor of Gershom Mott, colonel of the 6th New Jersey Volunteer Infantry, who rose to the rank of major general during the Civil War. It was manned from 1897 to 1922, and remained a military post until 1943. New Jersey acquired the site in 1947, opening it as a 106-acre state park in 1951.

Fort Delaware was also declared "surplus" by the federal government after World War II. It was opened as a Delaware state park in 1951. The island is about two-miles long and covers 178 acres. The state park contains an additional 110 acres on the Delaware shore (Temple, *The Union Prison at Fort Delaware*)

The Swamp Angel Comes to Trenton
by
Dr. David G. Martin

One of the most famous artillery pieces of the Civil War era was the Union "Swamp Angel" (also known as the "Marsh Battery"), an eight-ton monster that terrorized Charleston, South Carolina, for three days in August of 1863. The cannon, known technically as an eight-inch Parrott rifle, Model 1861, used a sixteen-pound powder charge to hurl a hundred-and-fifty pound shell as far as five miles, a range well beyond that of the Confederate artillery defending Charleston. The Swamp Angel was noted as much for the unique platform that supported it in a marsh at the southern edge of Charleston harbor as it was for its range. Union engineers used 13,000 sand bags, over 10,000 feet of planks and a force of 7000 men to construct the base that supported and protected the huge cannon.

The Swamp Angel in position after exploding in South Carolina. (David Martin)

After three weeks of strenuous labor, the Swamp Angel was ready to open fire at 1:30 A.M. on August 22, 1863. Its blasts startled the citizens of Charleston, who at first could not determine where the screeching shells were coming from. Fortunately for Charlestonians, the Swamp Angel was using experimental incendiary shells. One of these may have caused the gun to blow up at about 1:00 A.M. on August 24, 1863, as it fired its thirty-sixth round. This explosion caused the breech or rear part of the gun to blow out of its reinforcing band just behind the vent, making it unfit for further use. The explosion also threw the gun onto its parapet, making it appear to be ready to fire again, a fact that continued to distress the people of Charleston for some time.

At the end of its brief career, the now-famous Swamp Angel became only so much scrap metal and was junked along with other disabled cannons from the siege of Charleston. After the war, a pile of broken heavy artillery from Charleston was bought as scrap by Charles Carr of the Phoenix Iron Company of Trenton. When the shipment arrived in Trenton, a veteran who had served at Charleston claimed that he recognized the broken barrel of the Swamp Angel gun amidst the

Swamp Angel cannon monument on Perry Street in Trenton, circa 1900 (David Martin)

scrap. A man named John Hart Brewer suggested setting up the cannon as a monument, and succeeded at raising enough money to do so. A plot of land at the intersection of Clinton and Perry streets was donated by the city of Trenton, and the monument base itself was designed by Isaac Brougham of Trenton. It was constructed of Trenton brownstone in the shape of a truncated pyramid. The barrel was placed atop of the base "plain for all to see," and the monument was dedicated in February 1877. An article in the December 1, 1876, *New York Times* described the construction of the memorial, and early pictures of it show the date February 1877 on its identifying plaque. When the plaque was replaced at a subsequent date, the incorrect year of 1871 was accidentally inscribed.

The Swamp Angel was rededicated on December 3, 1915, and remained at the intersection of Clinton and Perry streets until the advent of the Civil War Centennial, when it had to be moved because of street modifications. It was transferred to its present location in Cadwallader Park and rededicated on April 12, 1961, when the principal speaker was Dr. Harold Morrison Smith, Headmaster of Bordentown Military Academy. Thirty-three years later the cannon and its base were cleaned by the Camp Olden Civil War Round Table. It was rededicated once more on October 8, 1994, with Dr. David Martin giving the rededication speech.

Swamp Angel at its present location in Cadwallader Park (Bruce Sirak)

There has been some controversy for a number of years as to whether or not the cannon in Trenton is, in fact, the genuine "Swamp Angel." In the 1970s, artillery historian Warren Ripley argued that at least six guns of the same size as the Swamp Angel were disabled near Charleston during the war, and that four of them blew off at the breech, the same spot where the Swamp Angel came apart. In the absence of serial numbers or other identifying marks, Ripley argued that there was only a one in four chance that Trenton's "Swamp Angel" was the real thing.

Recent research, however, seems to confirm that the gun in Trenton is indeed the original Swamp Angel. General Quincy A. Gilmore, commander of Union operations at Charleston, was a meticulous officer who carefully recorded the serial numbers of all his cannons. Gilmore's notes reveal that the cannon known as the Swamp Angel was stamped with serial number "6." Other evidence suggests that the gun in Trenton was cast at the West Point Foundry in New York in 1863 and weighed 16,577 pounds. It is now known that Ripley was not able to see the serial number on the gun during his assessment. Efforts to clean the muzzle since then have revealed the following markings: "No. 6/1xxx/W.P.F./8 IN." This information agrees in every way with Gilmore's notes and the notes from the foundry — that the Trenton gun is gun number "6," made at the West Pound Foundry (W.P.F.) and is an 8-incher. All that is lacking are the three last digits of its year of manufacture (1863). Also lacking, unfortunately, is the gun's distinctive breech band, common to all Parrott rifles, which apparently was lost in Charleston after the gun blew up or when the broken barrel was being transported to Trenton.

Trenton's cannon, then, is most likely the actual Swamp Angel, and as such it is a significant relic of the Civil War. It is also a controversial one. In 1960, 1988 and 1990, three different Trenton mayors proposed sending the gun back to Charleston as a "good will" token, a "grand gesture of reconciliation with the South." At least one of these officials seems to have been confused as to the actual role of the gun, mistaking it for the gun that fired the first shot of the Civil War at Fort Sumter. These attempts have been strongly and successfully opposed by local citizens, veterans' groups and Civil War enthusiasts at each juncture. An ideal use of the cannon would be as a centerpiece for a state museum on the Civil War or New Jersey history. Perhaps it even could be moved to the plaza in front of the New Jersey State Museum on State Street in downtown Trenton. (Stryker, "The Swamp Angel"; Ripley, *Artillery and Ammunition*: *New York Times*; Olmstead, Stark and Tucker, *The Big Guns*)

The Swamp Angel
by
Herman Melville

There is a coal-black Angel
  With a thick Afric lip,
And he dwells (like the hunted and harried)
  In a swamp where the green frogs dip.
But his face is against a City
  Which is over a bay of the sea,

And he breathes with a breath that is blastment,
    And dooms by a far decree.

By night there is fear in the City,
    Through the darkness a star soareth on;
There's a scream that screams up to the zenith,
    Then the poise of a meteor lone—
Lighting far the pale fright of the faces,
    And downward the coming is seen;
Then the rush, and the burst, and the havoc,
    And wails and shrieks between.

It comes like the thief in the gloaming;
    It comes, and none may foretell
The place of the coming—the glaring;
    They live in a sleepless spell
That wizens, and withers, and whitens;
    It ages the young, and the bloom
Of the maiden is ashes of roses—
    The Swamp Angel broods in his gloom.

Swift is his messengers' going,
    But slowly he saps their halls,
As if by delay deluding.
    They move from their crumbling walls
Farther and farther away;
    But the Angel sends after and after,
By night with the flame of his ray—
    By night with the voice of his screaming—
Sends after them, stone by stone,
    And farther walls fall, farther portals,
And weed follows weed through the Town.

Is this the proud City? the scorner
    Which never would yield the ground?
Which mocked at the coal-black Angel?
    The cup of despair goes round.

Vainly she calls upon Michael
    (The white man's seraph was he),
For Michael has fled from his tower
    To the Angel over the sea.

Who weeps for the woeful City
    Let him weep for our guilty kind;
Who joys at her wild despairing—
    Christ, the Forgiver, convert his mind.

Poem
by
"Joe Trenton" 1961
Published in a local paper

People of East Trenton,
  Please rally to my call.
Don't send me back to Charleston
  For I figured in the fall.

For a century I have guarded
  Your children and your gals,
The Laurels and the Tigers,
  St. Joseph's and your pals.

The Irish and the Germans,
  The Swedes and Polish too,
Have played beneath my shadow
  And fine Americans too.

A veteran of an old war.
  Whose fighters are all dead;
Should receive the help of someone
  For the sake of those ahead.

I love the town and people,
  The rich, the poor and all;
I want to stay in Trenton,
  And be at your beck and call.

So don't send me back to Charleston,
  As a prisoner of war.
Just keep me here in Trenton,
  Where I can help much more.

Hightstown Commemorates the War:
An Ordinary Monument with an Ironic Twist
by
Dr. David G. Martin

In 1861, Hightstown, New Jersey, was a sleepy agricultural community with a population of just under 1000. Located in eastern Mercer County, about fifteen miles east of the state capital at Trenton, the town's experiences during the war were no doubt similar to those of many small towns throughout the North.

The movement to construct a postwar monument to Hightstown's Civil War heroes began about a year after the close of the conflict. Inspiration may have been provided by the nearby Middlesex County town of Cranbury, then engaged in a similar project. Cranbury's effort proved more concerted, as its monument was dedicated in August 1866. Hightstown's monument committee, severely hampered by lack of funds, did not complete its memorial until 1875.

The Hightstown Soldiers' Monument Committee was created by the borough's Common Council on March 30, 1866. In April, the committee decided to raise money by holding "festivals" and by conducting a "general subscription" for individual donors. The first fund raiser was a lecture given at the Baptist Church in May 1866, and on the Fourth of July the committee sold refreshments at ceremonies held at the Presbyterian Church. Through these and similar projects, $1,000 was raised over the next eight years. This amount was still not enough to build a monument of suitable size, however, so the township voted in 1874 to raise an additional $1,200 by special taxation. Final plans for the monument were then prepared by the newly incorporated "East Windsor Soldiers' Monument Association."

Announcement of the Hightstown monument dedication (David Martin)

The contract to build the monument was awarded to John Ewart's Hightstown Marble Works, which crafted the whole memorial except for the life-sized eagle on its top. The monument was designed by Jacob P. Smith of Philadelphia and consists of a shaft twenty-three feet high made of Italian marble, resting on a granite base two feet high and five feet square. The sides of the shaft feature relief sculptures, which were said at the time to be first class and comparing favorably with work done in Italy. The reliefs consisted of seals of the United States, New Jersey and Mercer County, plus a life-size composition of a flag, a rifle modeled after one used by Thomas Scroggy of the 10th New Jersey Volunteer Infantry, and a sword modeled after one carried by Major T.B. Appleget of the 9th New Jersey Volunteer Infantry.

The monument was almost completed before a site for its location was agreed upon. It appears to have been originally slated for the town cemetery, but there was a popular outcry against this in the spring of 1875, with most people believing it should be placed in a more public location. Various spots were suggested, including the junction of the Trenton and Princeton Roads, on the old York Road, or at the junction of two major streets in town. Eventually a site was agreed on at the juncture of Stockton and Morrison Streets, on the road to Princeton near the edge of town.

The major inscription engraved on the monument's southeast face reads: "To the memory of the heroic volunteers of East Windsor Township who gave their lives as a sacrifice for their country and humanity, in the suppression of the Great Rebellion of 1861-65. This monument is erected by their grateful fellow citizens." Inscribed below this, and on two additional faces of the monument, are the names of thirty-five East Windsor soldiers, most, but not all, of whom died in the war. The list was first prepared by Major A.J. Smith in 1866, when 200 copies were printed and offered for sale to help raise money for the monument. A revised list of all the names, with complete service records, was published for public correction in the local newspaper on June 3, 1875.

The names on the monument are listed in two groups. On the northwest face are the names of 17 men who died in battle or in Confederate prison camps, arranged chronologically by order of death, with the exception of Lieutenant Voorhees Dye of the 1st New Jersey Volunteer Cavalry, who died in 1864 but is listed first because he was the town's only officer killed. On the southeast and northeast faces are the names of those who died of wounds or disease. Interestingly, at the end of the list are the names of a few soldiers who died between the end of the war and the erection of the monument in 1875. The concept of adding names of additional deaths as they occurred after the monument was dedicated was never carried out. For this reason the monument is not a complete record of the names of all the town's men who served in the Civil War.

Each soldier's unit is listed next to his name. Fourteen of the 35 listed belonged to Company A of the 6th New Jersey Volunteer Infantry (though two are listed as members of the 1st New Jersey Volunteer Infantry). Three Jemisons are listed (Peter, William and George), all of whom were casualties in the war. Research shows that four of the town's men died at the battle of Williamsburg, Virginia, on May 5, 1862, and four others were lost during the battle of Spotsylvania, Virginia, in May 1864. No less than five died in Confederate prisons: three at Andersonville in Georgia, one at Libby Prison in Richmond, and one, Charles A. Coward of the 10th New Jersey Volunteer Infantry, who was "murdered in the rebel prison at Lynchburg, Va., by a brutal guard, Oct. 1, 1864." A total of five of the soldiers listed fell victim to disease (chronic diarrhea, dysentery, fever and exposure); in reality, many more soldiers perished from disease than from battle. Nine of the soldiers listed survived the war

The monument was dedicated amidst impressive ceremonies on July 5, 1875. At 11 A.M. a lengthy parade, including several bands and veterans groups, and also carriages containing dignitaries, former officers, and the press, marched down Main Street. President Ulysses S. Grant had been invited but was unable to attend. The procession halted at the Baptist Church, where some officers spoke, and then proceeded to "Monument Square" for the unveiling of the monument. More music followed, along with a thirteen-gun salute and a speech by ex-governor Joel Parker, after which everyone adjourned to enjoy parties and picnics. It was, all in all, a quite splendid day for the town – and a remarkably sober one, as the town newspaper noted.

Hightstown's experience setting up its Civil War battle monument was doubtless typical of what hundreds, even thousands, of towns across the North (and South) were undergoing at the same time. The only major difference from the usual design was that the Hightstown monument featured an eagle made of Italian marble on the top, rather than the more common (and economical) "soldier at rest" statue so often used. It also wasn't unusual for towns to adorn their Civil War parks with war surplus cannon barrels supplied by the government, as Hightstown did. The town must have applied for some government surplus cannons early in their "monumentation" process, since evidence suggests that they may have had their artillery in hand by 1870, five years before the project was completed.

What was unusual in Hightstown's case, though, was the type of cannon barrels that the town received from the government. The guns delivered were not common six-pounders or twelve-pounder "Napoleons" or even the interesting Dahlgren boat howitzers that flank the Asbury Park monument. Instead, Hightstown received four magnificent looking rifled guns known as "Parrott rifles." Named after their inventor, Robert Parker Parrott, these cannon barrels had distinctive reinforcing bands around their breech (the base of the tube, opposite the end with the barrel). Rifled guns were usually classified by the diameter of their barrel (these are 2.9 inches) and the weight of their projectile (10 pounds).

The Hightstown monument and its cannons (David Martin)

Hightstown's four gun barrels lay innocently at the four corners of the monument for quite a number of years until someone finally took a closer look at their structure. It was then that at least two of the guns were discovered to be rare examples of Confederate-made Parrott rifles. To be precise, they are Parrotts made with "Brooke" features, which are variations made on the Parrott product by Confederate artificer John Mercer Brooke. This type of gun had the same general design as federal Parrott rifles but included a few modifications that the Confederates had to make because of their casting and construction capabilities. The Hightstown guns are much the same as their Union counterparts, but are longer and heavier. In addition, their barrels taper more than U.S. Parrotts, their reinforcing bands have a taper to them, and their lands and grooves ("rifling") are in the hook-slant form.

Hightstown's distinctive guns remained in their original location until 1978, when a representative of the Eaglehead Arsenal of Emmaus, Pennsylvania, offered to buy them from the town for $8000. A hue and cry arose among local citizens and patriotic groups against parting with part of the town's history for a temporary monetary windfall, and a special committee was set up under local historian Alphaeus Albert to study the cannons. While the town debated the purchase offer, the mayor had the barrels removed to storage for fear that someone would try to steal them. Eventually the purchase offer was refused – partly because of the local historical value of the guns and partly because their estimated value was thought to be much higher than the offer. The guns were returned to their accustomed spot the next spring, but were chained down for security.

The guns rested peaceably for another fifteen years until 1994, when a collector from Bryn Mawr, Pennsylvania, offered the town $40,000 for the four guns. Once again a public outcry arose. Once again the mayor removed the guns to storage while the town fathers debated their fate (this time they were sent to the town garage, next door to the police station and municipal court). A special committee composed of Larry Blake, Barry Clark and David Martin was appointed to set to work study and clean the cannons in order to try to confirm their identity.

The committee succeeded in proving that all four cannons were indeed rare Confederate-made Parrott rifles in the Brooke pattern. The barrels were found to weigh between 1,130 and 1,180 pounds each, matching the range of the other five known surviving cannons of this type. After layer on layer of old black paint was removed from the tubes, their serial numbers were discovered (1138, 1150, 1180 and 1182). These matched Confederate records from Richmond that showed the guns were cast between June 9, 1862, and November 19, 1863, by J.R. Anderson & Company ("J.R.A."), which was also known as the Tredegar Iron Works or Tredegar Foundry ("T.F.").

The confirmed identity of the cannons only served to heighten the debate about whether to sell them or not. New Jersey artillery expert Neil Friedenthal contacted the town council to advise them that the cannons were worth much more than $10,000 each – perhaps as much as $25,000 to $35,000 each. In reply, the man who made the original offer, Russell Pritchard III, said that the cannons would be very expensive to restore; then he sweetened the pot by offering to replace them with reproduction barrels and carriages. He even claimed that he would keep them at his home and later donate them to a museum. Some townspeople were ready to sell the guns at any price in order to help out the town's cash-strapped budget.

Other residents campaigned vigorously to keep the cannons as part of the history of the town. Borough historian Clark Hutchinson asked: "Do we sell our heritage to appease taxpayers?" And another citizen asked, "What will they sell next year, the marble Civil War monument?"

In the end, the town's heritage, and New Jersey's, won out. The cannons were not sold, and they were returned to their accustomed spot, with even stronger chains to hold them down. They were rededicated on the Fourth of July, and hopefully will not have to be moved again. Incidentally, the last potential buyer, who promised to keep them at his home and then donate them to a museum, pled guilty eight years later to numerous instances of fraud in connection with cases involving other Civil War artifacts. (Orr, "Reflections from the Shrine"; Martin, "Hightstown in the Civil War"; bit.ly/LincolnClassRoom)

The Second Coming of Hackettstown's "Billy Yank"
by
Gilbert "Skip" Riddle

Hackettstown, New Jersey, lies nestled alongside the Musconetcong River among the rolling hills of Warren County. During the Civil War, the little town contributed troops to a number of New Jersey units. In the waning days of the 19th century, Hackettstown's citizens decided to follow the lead of many other municipalities in the state and erect a monument to their men who had fought for the Union.

The original Hackettstown "Billy Yank" atop his fountain/pedestal (Gilbert "Skip" Riddle)

The committee appointed to select and acquire the monument decided to order a generic "soldier at rest" from the catalog of the J. W. Fiske Iron Works of New York City. Fiske created statues from a variety of materials, and the committee chose one of cast zinc, finished with a bronzed patina. The statue's $700 cost was raised from several sources. The town council provided $200, another $300 was raised by local schoolchildren, who donated their pocket change to the effort, and the remaining $200 was contributed by local businessmen. The completed statue was placed atop a nineteen-foot-tall pedestal on lower Main Street (today's Route 46). The lower level of the monument featured a water fountain for humans as well as a zinc horse head spewing water into bowls designed for use by local horses and dogs.

Hackettstown's dual purpose "public drinking fountain and soldiers' monument" was dedicated with much hoopla at 11:00 A.M. on "Decoration Day" (today's Memorial Day), May 30, 1896. Local dignitaries led a parade to the site headed by the Hackettstown cornet band, followed by local fraternal organizations, fire departments and a bevy of schoolchildren waving American flags. There was also a large turnout of spectators "… [who] braved a rainstorm to attend the dedicatory oration delivered by the Rev. J.C. Chapman, pastor of the Presbyterian Church." Following the ceremony, the parade reformed and marched to Vernon Hall, where dinner was served.

Photographs of the monument, popularly known locally as "Billy Yank," reveal that it was located in the middle of the street without any protective barriers or fencing around it. This placement proved troublesome with the advent of 20th-century automobile and truck traffic. The state of New Jersey built a concrete highway, Route 46, through the town and around the monument in 1922, but by 1926, with the highway about to be widened, state officials decided, apparently with no protest on the part of the town government, that evolving traffic patterns made it "best to have the monument removed."

No documentation by town or state records detailing what actually happened survive, but according to local lore, Wednesday, December 29, 1926, was Billy Yank's last day. Either New Jersey Department of Transportation workers or private contractors tied one end of a rope around the monument and the other end to a truck and toppled it. The fragile zinc statue fractured in numerous places and the remains were swept up and sold for scrap. On January 14, 1927, the *Hackettstown Gazette* published Schooley's Mountain poet Augustus Stewart Gulick's mournful laudatory verses on Billy Yank's fate. They read, in part:

> But alas, here comes the junk man with a stout rope.
> He has pulled me to the concrete and my back is broke.
> Where are the citizens of yester-year
> Who placed me here with lusty cheers.
> I think the citizens of Hackettstown
> Could at least have gently taken me down.
> I was a memorial to the boys of sixty-five,
> But few of them are now alive.
> Who remembers the famous day and year,
> When the patriots of Hackettstown placed me here.
> The boys it seems are now forgotten
> As I lie in a junk pile to rust and rotten.

Since the statue had been erected some three decades prior, it is safe to assume that many of the "citizens of yesteryear," especially those schoolchildren who contributed their lunch money as the largest donation to the cost of the monument, were indeed still around. Protest, however, appears to have been minimal. It was a different era.

Not everyone was indifferent. Some scooped up fragments as souvenirs. Probably the only piece of the Billy Yank monument still extant today is the water-spewing horse head, salvaged from the scrap pile by one Fred Thomas, who thought the destruction of the monument "a crime." Thomas later passed the head on to local merchant Louis Hart. Louis' son Bill painted the horse head gold, and it currently hangs, along with other local historical memorabilia, including old postcards and a plate decorated with a picture of the monument, on the wall of his County Line Sports Shop in Hackettstown.

In the late 1990s, Henry Monetti of Great Meadows read the story of the monument's destruction at the local library. Monetti was appalled, and launched a campaign to have the state of New Jersey replace it, since it was torn down as part of a state construction project. Monetti energetically sought support for his cause everywhere he could, sending letters to anyone he thought might be able to aid in the effort, from President Bill Clinton and Governor Christine Whitman to local politicians and historical societies. He enlisted Hackettstown musician Kevin McCann to compose a tune about the statue that was played by the "Colonial Musketeers," a local fife and drum corps. Monetti was soon joined in his quest by Howard Niper and Charles Prestopine. Prestopine established and chaired a committee to raise money to replace the monument. The committee, which Prestopine recalled as "a true community effort," eventually raised $50,000 from local sources, and Prestopine himself testified before the New Jersey State Assembly budget committee. As a result, Assemblyman Leonard Lance, with the support of Assemblywoman Connie Myers and State Senator William Schluter, included the remaining $100,000 in necessary funding in New Jersey's Fiscal Year 2000/2001 budget.

Money in hand, Prestopine contacted sculptor Michael Kraus, who had taken on such tasks previously, to create an authentic bronze duplicate of the original zinc Billy Yank. In a remarkable stroke of luck, Kraus had access to an original 19th-century mold used to create the generic statues that adorned so many monuments, including Hackettstown's. Buddy Slifkin of the Keystone Memorial Company coordinated materials and contractors to prepare the remainder of the monument, and on May 26, 2001, the new Billy was lifted by crane atop the twelve-foot-high prepared pedestal, which was engraved with the names of major battles and a poem, "Remember You Are Jerseymen." It also bore two polished black-granite panels featuring a Gettysburg battle scene and an American eagle and United States flag. A replica of a horse's head and a bas-relief water basin completed the base and commemorated the original dual purpose of the monument. Once Billy was lowered into place, the proprietor of nearby David's Country Inn brought out champagne and strawberries to help the crew celebrate the successful installation.

Billy Yank's replacement in Hackettstown (Gilbert "Skip" Riddle)

The new Billy Yank monument was dedicated on May 28, 2001. Unfortunately, Henry Monetti and Howard Niper, so instrumental in initiating the campaign to restore the Hackettstown monument, did not live to see their dream become reality. The day proved cloudy and rainy, not unlike that of the original dedication back in 1926. Over a thousand people attended, however, and in a striking bit of symbolism, the cloud cover cleared and the sun shone down on Billy as the dedication commenced. As the ceremony ended, the clouds rolled in and it began to rain once more. But no matter, for Billy Yank had returned to Hackettstown. (Snell, *History of Warren and Sussex Counties; Warren Reporter; Star- Ledger*; Interviews with Dr. Carol Grissom, Michael Kraus, Alan Gibson, Buddy Slifkin, Charles Prestopine, Charles Riddle and Karl Jensen)

The Jerseymen and the Plow Boys
by
Gilbert "Skip" Riddle

The 9th New Jersey Volunteer Infantry was organized at Trenton's Camp Olden in the autumn of 1861 and left for Washington D.C., on December 4. The 9th was enlisted as a "rifle regiment" from among the state's best shots, including German target shooters from Newark. With a large number of Jersey Shore "watermen" in the ranks as well, the regiment was a natural choice for Major General Ambrose Burnside's North Carolina expedition, organized to conduct an amphibious assault on Cape Hatteras in early 1862. Unfortunately, the 9th lost its colonel, Joseph W. Allen, and surgeon, Frederick S. Weller, who both drowned when their small boat overturned during landing operations on January 30. Lieutenant Colonel Heckman, a former conductor on the Pennsylvania Railroad, assumed command and was promoted to colonel. The 9th subsequently participated in the battle of Roanoke Island on February 8, where the men of the regiment gained the nickname "Jersey Muskrats" for their ability to push through a swamp in a successful attack on Confederate positions. A less positive outcome of the battle was the death of the 9th's Captain Joseph Henry, the first New Jersey officer to die in battle in the Civil War, when he was hit in the chest by a spent cannon ball.

After capturing Roanoke Island, Burnside pushed on to the mainland with the objective of capturing the coastal rail center of New Bern (then known as New Berne). The Union assault force disembarked at the mouth of Slocum Creek on March 13, with regimental bands aboard ships blaring in the background as the men clambered out of boats and waded ashore through mud to firmer ground in an unopposed landing operation. Although there was no fighting, the 9th New Jersey suffered one casualty as Private Michael B. Reading of Company C drowned in the Neuse River. Once ashore, General Burnside's army marched twelve miles north in a torrential rain that turned clay roads into a quagmire, and camped for the night without tents in the mud.

In the March 18 attack on New Bern's defenses, the 9th New Jersey held the left flank of the federal line, with the 21st Massachusetts Volunteer Infantry deployed to the regiment's right. The Rebel entrenchments opposite them were manned by the 26th North Carolina Regiment under Colonel Zebulon Vance, along with Captain Henry Harding's Independent Company of North Carolina infantry and some artillery. The New Jersey riflemen laid down a heavy and accurate suppressive fire on the enemy position, driving the Confederate artillerymen away from their guns. Although an attack by the 21st was repulsed, a Union breakthrough on the right unhinged the enemy line, the 9th rushed forward in a charge, and the remaining Rebels, under pressure from front and rear, ran for their lives. Colonel Heckman was the first Jerseyman in the Confederate position, and later reported that the regiment had captured "two officers, and several privates, and a rebel flag with this inscription, 'Beaufort Plow Boys.' It is in a good state of preservation, and will be kept so by the Ninth…" The Jerseymen lost 4 men killed and 58 wounded in the fight; 8 of the wounded would die of their injuries in the weeks ahead.

The 9th would spend most of the rest of the war in North Carolina, a unique assignment among New Jersey regiments. Within a month, however, the Beaufort Plow Boys flag was on display as New Jersey's first war trophy in the statehouse at Trenton. The "Beaufort Plow Boys" were the men of Captain Harding's company, whose flag had been made by the captain's sister and her friends in Beaufort and presented to the company at a ceremony in Chocowinity, North Carolina, the previous November. J. Madison Drake, the 9th New Jersey's historian, albeit with a bit of Victorian-era overwriting, described the banner thusly:

> The flag captured in the left battery by Company B, was quite handsome—its dimensions being three feet by six feet. It was emblazoned with thirteen stars, and bore the inscription— "Beaufort Plowboys, presented by the ladies of Beaufort." ... The stars that were radiant when Beaufort's maidens embroidered its azure field had become dim by the stains of battle. The once white and red cross, typical of purity and faith, had been torn by Jerseymen's bullets it had invited.

The 9th New Jersey monument in New Bern (Joseph Bilby)

In the early 20th century, New Jersey state officials decided to erect a monument to the 9th New Jersey, a neglected unit until then, at New Bern. On March 1, 1904, a bill appropriating the sum of five-thousand dollars for that purpose was introduced in the state senate by Senator William J. Bradley of Camden County. The bill was unanimously passed by both houses of the legislature and signed by Governor Franklin Murphy, himself a Civil War veteran who had served as a junior officer in the 13th New Jersey Volunteer Infantry. The site chosen for the granite monument was New Bern National Cemetery, where 53 men of the regiment were buried during the years the 9th served there. The legislature also allocated funds to locate and transport surviving veterans of the regiment to New Bern (an estimated 120 were still alive in 1904) so that they could be present at the dedication. In a gesture of good will, in keeping with the feeling of national reconciliation of the era, the legislature also approved returning the captured flag to the surviving members of the Beaufort Plow Boys.

On the day of the dedication, May 17, 1905, New Bern held a public reception for the visitors from New Jersey at the town's courthouse. The flag of the Beaufort Plow Boys was returned by New Jersey Assembly Speaker J. Boyd Avis, representing then New Jersey Governor Edward C. Stokes. After a brief speech, Avis unfurled the flag and presented it to Governor Robert B. Glenn of North Carolina to a round of applause by the local Sons and Daughters of the Confederacy.

Captain Harding, whose company had carried the flag before it ended up in New Jersey, was still alive, but decidedly unreconciled. He did not attend the ceremony because he believed that "... on account that cattle, furniture, and many precious items were stolen by those damned Yankees, they may as well keep the flag." His son, Fordyce C. Harding, a Spanish American War veteran, was more amenable and accepted the flag in his

Beaufort Plow Boys flag (North Carolina Museum of History)

father's stead. The younger Harding was accompanied by several of the women who had originally presented the flag to his father. Harding spoke a few words, in the spirit of the reconciliation movement: "On behalf of the survivors of the Beaufort Plow Boys, permit me to express the deepest feelings of love and veneration for the battle flag you have placed in my hands tonight, and to assure you that it is received with great pleasure...I am glad that I am the son of a Confederate veteran." The group then adjourned to the local Sons of Confederate Veterans hall for lunch.

In 1952, Harding donated the Plowboy flag to Chocowinity High School, where it remained on display for the next eighteen years, encased in a mahogany frame purchased by the senior class. The flag remained on display at the school until 1970, when it was transferred to the collections of the North Carolina Museum of History in Raleigh, where it remains to this day.

The Jerseymen of the 9th returned the flag they captured so many years before, but while they were in New Bern one of them picked up another, far more personal, souvenir of that long ago fight to bring back to the state in exchange. While wandering across the old New Bern battlefield, veteran James V. Clark of Cape May, who had served with Company D, found his old canteen, which he had lost there 43 years before during the wild charge towards the Confederate fortifications. And so things came full circle. (Drake, *Ninth New Jersey*; Martin, *Beaufort County Heroes*; *Report of the New Jersey State Commission*; conversation with Ed Harding)

Governor Franklin Murphy and New Jersey Assembly Speaker J. Boyd Avis. Avis spoke at the New Bern dedication. (Joseph Bilby)

Twilight of the Grand Army
by
S. Thomas Summers

Atlantic City, NJ - September 22-23, 1910

Last time I travelled this far south,
I was marching from Trenton
with New Jersey's 8th. Had a musket
on my shoulder and buttons gold
as Glory's streets. I also had the itch,
itch to fight, to burry steel and lead into the hearts
of every Johnny I saw. Guess I got to do just that:
Gettysburg, Fredericksburg, Savage Station.
In Virginia, Reb took my arm, but I got my wife back.
God gave us two boys and I rediscovered what life was,
life without war. Rebs I killed – all they got was blood and hell.

I'm not strong enough to fire a musket now,
got wrinkles deep as canyons,
and if Gen. Hooker ordered me to charge
through might and mire, I'd say no thank you, sir.
My bones creak like a tired oak in a windstorm,
but this salty air rubs on me nice. It's kinda scraping
the rest of the war off me and the ocean sings
a song as sweet as a church hymn on a cool Sunday morning.

My brothers are coming – brothers who fought,
bled, and cried right along with me.
Brothers who remember the faces of the Rebs they killed.
Tonight, I'll embrace those men –
we're all gonna cry one more time.

Grand Army of the Republic veterans form up for a parade in Atlantic City to kick off their 44th National Encampment, the only one held in New Jersey, in 1910. (David Hann)

New Jersey's Civil War Centennial Commission
by
Henry F. Ballone and Joseph G. Bilby

The National Civil War Centennial Commission (NCWCC) was established in 1957 by an act of Congress (Public Law 85-305). With limited appropriated funds to accomplish a major mission, the NCWCC members hoped that each state and locality would plan and engage in commemorating its own participation in the Civil War, the greatest national crisis in American history. The main thrust of the commission's centennial concept was to promote the ideal of a great and now united America, which had evolved out of the struggles of the 1860s, and support state and local efforts on that theme.

Southern states, of course, held the vast majority of battle sites, but New Jersey was a major manufacturing center during the conflict and enlisted many thousands of soldiers in the war effort. The state's heroes left a trail of marked and unmarked graves from Bull Run to Appomattox, and so, in 1959, the New Jersey Assembly and Senate passed, and Governor Robert B. Meyner signed, Joint Resolution Number 11, authorizing the New Jersey Civil War Centennial Commission (NJCWCC). The commission was initially composed of two state senators, two assemblymen and four citizens appointed at large. A subsequent resolution raised the number of citizen members by four and made provision for a paid executive director and assistant. Commission members served without compensation.

Governor Meyner proclaimed February 21, 1961, as the official opening day of Civil War centennial observances in New Jersey. At a joint legislative session that day, actor Anthony Quinn, portraying Abraham Lincoln, reenacted the president-elect's original address to the same body on the same day and hour a century earlier, speaking at the same lectern that Lincoln had used. A guest of honor at the ceremony was 103-year-old John W. Harris, who had been born a slave.

The New Jersey centennial commission considered its main message to be proclaiming the national ideals that had emerged from the strife of the Civil War, rather than staging reenactments of battles. A *Trentonian* editorial noted at the commission's advent that: "Re-staging battles would be all right if all the bitterness had

103-year-old John Harris, born a slave, listens to Anthony Quinn reenact President Lincoln's visit to the NJ Legislature in February 1961. (Ellis/*Steps in a Journey*)

141

New Jerseyans who reenacted the first battle of Bull Run. (John Kuhl)

evaporated with the passing of years, but anyone who has spent time in the deep South knows that such is not the case." On June 6, 1960, commission chairman Donald Flamm responded, telling a reporter that: "We in New Jersey are more interested in glorifying the great ideas which grew out of the costliest military experience our nation has ever had. In addition to preserving the Union, the Civil War brought about a greater understanding of the sectional and racial differences which caused it. It is these ideas we want to commemorate, and extend, if possible." With that in mind, the commission set itself four primary goals to accomplish during the four years of its existence:

1. "To achieve lasting values from the Centennial, notably an improved understanding and unity within our Nation, section by section and race by race."

Members of the N.J. Civil War Centennial Commission look at documents and other memorabilia relating to New Jersey's role in the Civil War. Seated (left to right) are Donald Flamm of Closter, commission chairman, and State Senator Sido L. Ridolfi of Trenton. Standing in the background are Edgar W. Smith of Morristown and Attorney General David D. Furman of Bedminster. (Somerset *Messenger Gazette*)

The NCWCC chose Charleston, South Carolina, as the site of its fourth National Assembly, to be held April 11-12, 1961, and invited commissions from states around the country, including New Jersey, to attend ceremonies commemorating the hundredth anniversary of the beginning of the war in Charleston. One of the New Jersey commissioners, former assemblywoman Mrs. Madaline Williams, was an African-American. The New Jerseyans were advised that while the white members of the delegation would be housed at the Francis Marion Hotel, the NCWCC headquarters, Mrs. Williams would have to stay in a separate, segregated, hotel. The mayor of Charleston advised the Jerseyans that if Mrs. Williams appeared at the Francis Marion it would be "very embarrassing to all concerned."

Predawn arrival of New Jersey delegation in Charleston caused a flurry on the railway platform. Officials of the National Association for the Advancement of Colored People are among the first to greet Everett J. Landers, executive director; Joseph N. Dempsey, vice chairman, and Assemblywoman Mrs. Madaline A. Williams, all of the New Jersey Civil War Centennial Commission. (Ellis/*Steps in a Journey*)

The centennial occurred as the Civil Rights movement, fueled by the 1954 *Brown versus Board of Education* Supreme Court decision ordering desegregation in Southern schools, began to pick up steam. In the spring of 1961 there were a number of anti-segregation "sit ins" at facilities throughout the South. In response to the overt discrimination evidenced in the case of Mrs. Williams, the New Jersey centennial commission adopted a resolution stressing that the commission's goal was to highlight American contributions to "human freedom, justice, and the dignity of the individual." The resolution pointed out that the Charleston event was being sponsored by a federally funded national commission, which was honor bound not to tolerate a situation where "custom and/or law . . . forbids equal hospitality to members of the Negro race . . ." The commission believed accepting such strictures would "abrogate . . . the fundamental concepts of human decency and the fundamental guarantees of civil liberties under the New Jersey Constitution . . ."

The New Jersey commission's stand was seconded by similar resolutions from the state's Senate and General Assembly, and quickly became national news. New Jersey Republican Senator Clifford Case informed Major General Ulysses S. Grant III, chairman of the NCWCC, that the senator supported the commission's stand, and Newark Democratic Congressman Hugh J. Addonizio read a resolution protesting the denial of hotel accommodations to Mrs. Williams into the Congressional Record. In response, South Carolina Democratic Governor Ernest F. Hollings claimed that New Jersey was playing politics and Chairman John May of the South Carolina Confederate Centennial Commission promised that his commission would "uphold the customs and laws of our state."

The matter escalated to consideration by a higher authority, and became the new Kennedy administration's first civil-rights test. A letter from President John F. Kennedy to General Grant pointed out that "as a governmental body the Commission had an obligation to provide equal treatment to those attending its meetings." Phone lines buzzed between Washington, General Grant's home, and Charleston as Grant tried to pressure the Francis Marion Hotel to "work something out." Northern newspapers editorialized in favor of the stand taken by the New Jersey commission while Southern papers, unsurprisingly, were sympathetic to South Carolina's position. The *Shreveport* (Louisiana) *Times* remarked: "Let's be honest. We are memorializing a bloody war that settled nothing except the question of who was strongest." What this had to do with the logic of racial discrimination in lodging in 1961 went unanswered.

Monument to the 23rd NJ Volunteer Infantry at Salem Church (Henry F. Ballone)

When negotiations failed to provide a non-segregated local site, the White House offered a naval base in Charleston. Two luncheons were held on the first day of the meeting — one at the naval base, sponsored by the national commission, and one at the Francis Marion Hotel, sponsored by the South Carolina commission. It was not an auspicious advent for the four-year centennial observances, but the Jerseyans had made their public point.

The following month, the monument to the 23rd New Jersey Volunteer Infantry at Salem Church, Virginia, was rededicated. On a rainy May 6, 1961, the New Jersey commission returned a Confederate battle flag captured a century prior to a representative of the state of Virginia. The monument commemorated was initially erected under the auspices of the New Jersey Legislature in 1907, forty-four years after the 23rd fought the 9th Alabama Infantry in a bloody encounter around the church and a nearby schoolhouse in May 1863. In less than half an hour the Jerseymen, southern Jersey boys, many from Burlington County, lost 119 men killed, wounded and missing in what would be a failing effort. The monument was erected during the early 20th-century "reconciliation" movement and one of the plaques mounted on it bears the words, "To the Brave Alabama Boys, Our Opponents on This Field of Battle, Whose Memory We Honor, This Tablet Is Dedicated." The text prompted the New Jersey commission to use the rededication to illustrate the "mutual affection and respect so frequently held by opposing forces during the Civil War . . . in contrast to the all-too-frequent emphasis on combat and slaughter." The commissioners hoped the ceremony would serve as a unifying event following the unpleasantness at Charleston, although Alabama failed to send representatives. This time, however, Mrs. Williams was uneventfully included in a box lunch served within the normally segregated church. The road to racial justice would be long and hard, with many bumps along the way, north and south, but the New Jersey Civil War Centennial Commission helped provide a beginning.

Rededicating the monument to the 15th NJ Volunteer infantry at Spotsylvania, 1964. (John Kuhl)

2. "To develop source materials within New Jersey such as diaries, letters, photographs, old newspapers and other memorabilia, in order to enhance historical awareness of New Jersey's roll in the Civil War."

One of the earliest projects of the New Jersey Civil War Centennial Commission was to advertise in the media in an effort to encourage state residents to search for unpublished New Jersey Civil War primary sources, including letters, manuscripts and diaries. Chairman Flamm declared that the Rutgers State University Library would serve as the commission's official repository for any such material discovered by New Jerseyans as a result of the campaign. The initiative proved an important one, saving valuable material from loss or destruction. Among the important research materials donated to Rutgers as a result of this project were the letters of Captain Ellis Hamilton of the 15th New Jersey Volunteer Infantry, the youngest Union officer to serve in the Civil War.

3. "To commemorate the efforts of the 88,305 New Jerseyans who fought in 26 major engagements from Bull Run to Appomattox, and to focus attention on those who distinguished themselves on both sides of the conflict."

Earl Schenck Miers, director of Rutgers University Press, popular history author and a member of the NJCWCC, opined that the dearth of published material on New Jersey's role in the Civil War in the years prior to the centennial was due to the fact that New Jersey had a "guilty conscience," over the state's history during the era. Miers claimed New Jersey was an "ambivalent" Union state, and as evidence noted that there were still slaves in New Jersey in 1860, that the state did not give all its electoral votes to Lincoln and that New Jerseyans thought of themselves as citizens of a "border state."

One could just as easily, and probably more accurately, posit that the lack of recent books on New Jersey Civil War history in 1961 was simply due to disinterest. New Jersey was flooded with immigrants, most of whom had no family connection with the conflict, in the century following the war. In addition New Jersey became a modern industrial society in the 20th century, with a tendency to look forward rather than back. It should also be noted that much of Miers' assessment of Civil War era politics in New Jersey was no doubt based on the dubious study by Charles M. Knapp, *New Jersey Politics During the Period of Civil War and Reconstruction*. Dr. William Gillette's more recent *Jersey Blue* has provided a much-needed corrective to Knapp's conclusions. Although it had its problems with the Lincoln administration and its policies, New Jersey's loyalty to the Union cause was never in doubt.

Perhaps as a balance, Miers attempted to stimulate pride in New Jersey's military role in the war, stating that New Jerseyans should be proud of the "88,305 troops the state supplied to the Union, far exceeding its quota by more than 10,000 without a draft." He also wanted the state's youth to become aware of heroes like Generals Philip Kearny, Gershom Mott and Hugh Judson Kilpatrick. To that end, the NJCWCC published a booklet entitled *New Jersey in the Civil War & Civil War Facts*, which included information regarding the state's participation in the war, including a listing of military units, statistics on casualties and costs of the war, and brief notes on personalities. A more substantive contribution was the publication of the letters of Colonel Robert McAllister, edited by Dr. James I. Robertson and published through the sponsorship of the commission by Rutgers University Press in 1965.

In actuality, Miers was as much in error in his overall military conclusions as in his political ones. The true number of New Jerseyans who served in the Civil War will probably never be known, but it is lower than Miers, quoting late 19th-century sources, suggested. Federal government figures credit the state, including navy and marine enlistments, with a total of 78,817 men. Some of these were reenlisting veterans from 1864 who were counted twice, which reduces the total to 75,863. Other reenlistments are impossible to tally, but did exist in fairly large numbers. And, despite Miers' claim, there was, of course, conscription in New Jersey; a small state draft for nine-months-service troops was held in 1862 and larger federally organized drafts took place in 1864. Miers' use of General Kilpatrick as a potential role model for youngsters is, to say the least, puzzling – but there is no doubt he meant well.

4. "To encourage and coordinate, where possible, local observances in various communities in the state, and to rededicate long-forgotten monuments which were raised in memory of New Jersey soldiers in other states."

Civil War centennial programs were held throughout the state at venues such as Fairleigh Dickinson University, where panel discussions on slavery and a talk by commission member and New Jersey Attorney General David D. Furman on Lincoln's 1861 visit to the state was coupled with an exhibition drill by members of the 2nd New Jersey Volunteer Infantry North-South Skirmish Association (N-SSA) unit. The commission declared the N-SSA's 15th New Jersey Volunteer Infantry the official honor guard for the centennial, and the 15th participated in Civil War uniform in commission events, as well as representing New Jersey in several battle reenactments.

Earl Schenck Miers addressed the New Brunswick Historical Club in 1963 on the subject of the Emancipation Proclamation and New Jersey, noting that the state's 25,000 free African-Americans were not free to send their children to school or vote in the state by the document. It was not until March 31, 1870 – one day after the ratification of the 15th Amendment – that Thomas Mundy of Perth Amboy, New Jersey, became the first black American to vote under its auspices.

In addition to Salem Church, the NJCWCC conducted out-of-state rededications of New Jersey Civil War monuments at Antietam, Maryland, Ox Hill, Virginia and the Philip Kearny grave site in Arlington National Cemetery in 1962; Gettysburg, where the commission dedicated a concrete bench at the original First New Jersey Brigade monument, in 1963; and Fredericksburg and Spotsylvania, Virginia, and Monocacy, Maryland, in 1964.

All in all, the commission had accomplished its goals, in increasingly trying times, as the nation faced new challenges and turbulent changes at home while a new war, far more ambiguous than the one it was commemorating, loomed on the horizon. (Cook, *Troubled Commemoration*; Bilby & Goble, *Remember You Are Jerseymen*: Gillette, *Jersey Blue*; Centennial Commission File, NJ State Archives)

The reactivated 15th NJ Volunteer Infantry reenacting the battle of Hanover, Pennsylvania, in 1963. (John Kuhl)

The Authors

Henry F. Ballone is retired as owner and operator of a firm making film for printers and is currently a photojournalist and graphic designer. He is Vice President of the Lincoln Group of New York and a member of the New Jersey Civil War Heritage Association and its 150th Anniversary Committee, the Board of Advisors of the Lincoln Forum, the Executive Boards of the Phil Kearny and Robert E. Lee Civil War Round Tables as well as a member of other Lincoln and Civil War organizations. He is the graphic designer of the Lincoln Forum "Bulletin," Lincoln Group of New York "Wide Awake," and several books, including this series. His Lincoln and Civil War photos are posted at: web.me.com/civilwarnut

John G. Bilby received his BA and MA degrees in history from Rutgers University, where he was ROTC battalion commander and graduated Phi Beta Kappa. He is a first lieutenant in the New Jersey National Guard and is pursuing studies for a teaching certificate at the City University of New York. He currently lives in Manhattan with his wife Carol Mendez, a family physician, and two dogs.

Joseph G. Bilby received his BA and MA degrees in history from Seton Hall University, served as a first lieutenant in the First Infantry Division in the Vietnam War and is the author or editor of thirteen books on New Jersey and military history, including *Remember You Are Jerseymen* with William Goble, *Small Arms at Gettysburg* and *Freedom to All: New Jersey's African American Civil War Soldiers*. Retired from the New Jersey Department of Labor as Supervising Investigator, he is a trustee of the New Jersey Civil War Heritage Association, website and publications editor for its 150th Anniversary Committee and assistant curator of the National Guard Militia Museum of New Jersey in Sea Girt.

Thomas R. Burke, Jr. is a trustee of the New Jersey Civil War Heritage Association and member of its 150th Anniversary Committee. He has been active in the Civil War reenacting community for many years and is currently a member of the Winfield Scott Hancock Society, the 69th NYSVHA, the 6th New York Independent Battery and the 13th New Jersey Volunteer Infantry. He has been published in *Civil War Historian* magazine and contributed to National Park Service documentary projects.

Bruce M. Form received a BA in history from Athens State University and an MA in behavioral science from Kean State University. He is a retired Woodbridge Township high school vice principal, member of the executive committee of the Robert E. Lee Civil War Round Table and executive director of the Round Table's Civil War Library and Research Center. Mr. Form and his wife, Mira Katz Form, are students of the role of Jews in the Civil War, and he portrays Captain Myer Asch of the 1st New Jersey Cavalry in living history presentations.

Robert Gerber received BS degrees in Marketing and Accounting and an MBA in Finance from Fairleigh Dickinson University and is retired from the banking industry. He is a member of the New Jersey Civil War Heritage Association's 150th Anniversary Committee as well as vice president of the Phil Kearny Civil War Round Table, Wayne, New Jersey. He is also a member of the Little Big Horn Associates and the Custer Battlefield Historical & Museum Association.

Steven D. Glazer received his BA, BSEE and JD degrees from Rutgers University, and an MS from Fairleigh Dickinson University. Mr. Glazer retired as a lieutenant colonel in the USAR in 1997, after serving six years as an intelligence/electronic-warfare officer in the Pentagon. He is a partner of the law firm of Weil, Gotshal & Manges LLP and adjunct professor of law at Rutgers. He is also author of *Discover Your Community's Civil War Heritage.*

William E. Hughes received his BA degree in history from Pfeiffer University, Misenheimer, North Carolina and an M.Ed from West Chester University, West Chester, Pennsylvania. A retired teacher of 38 years experience and current local school board member, he is also secretary of the Old Baldy Civil War Round Table of Philadelphia and author of a number of articles for that organization's newsletter. He has also published The Civil War Papers of his great-great grandfather, Lt. Col. Newton T. Colby of the 107th New York Volunteer Infantry.

Valerie M. Josephson received her BA degree from George Washington University and edited a medical journal for many years. Her great-grandfather was seriously wounded during the Civil War, spurring her interest in Civil War medicine. She is currently writing a book on the nine surgeons of the four New Jersey Militia regiments.

John W. Kuhl is a graduate of Penn State University who spent three years as a US Navy deck officer and navigator in the Antarctic during the 1950s. A lifelong student and leading collector of New Jersey related Civil War relics and photographs and author of articles on the state's soldiers, he is retired from an agricultural career in his native Hunterdon County, New Jersey.

Robert F. MacAvoy, a USAF Vietnam veteran, retired in 2002 as a senior supervisor/project engineer for Merck & Company, Rahway, New Jersey. He is co-author, with Charles Eckhardt, of *Our Brothers Gone Before*, an inventory of Civil War veteran burials in New Jersey, and is currently searching for the names of over 10,000 veterans who may be buried in New Jersey cemeteries in addition to the 41,000 already discovered, as well as out-of-state burials of veterans with ties to New Jersey.

James M. Madden received his BA in Marketing from Saint Peter's College in Jersey City, New Jersey and has contributed articles to many Civil War publications and projects. A political consultant, he is also a trustee of the New Jersey Civil War Heritage Association and its 150th Anniversary Committee, a trustee of the Historic Jersey City and Harsimus Cemetery, a member of the Association of Professional Genealogists (APGEN) and a Trustee for the Jerramiah T. Healy Charitable Foundation for a Better Jersey City.

Dr. David G. Martin received his BA from the University of Michigan and holds MA and PhD degrees from Princeton University. He is a teacher and administrator at the Peddie School, president of the New Jersey Civil War Heritage Association, a member of its 150th Anniversary Committee and publisher/editor of Longstreet House book company. Dr. Martin is author and editor of a number of works on the Civil War, including *Gettysburg, July 1* and *Jackson's Valley Campaign*, and on New Jersey's role in the war, including *The Monocacy Regiment*.

Sylvia Mogerman has a BA in elementary and secondary English education and was a teacher for over thirty years. She is now editor, publicist and board member of the Phil Kearny Civil War Round Table, board member and historian for the League of Historical Societies of New Jersey, a member of the New Jersey Civil War Heritage Association's 150th Anniversary Committee and a volunteer for Golden Retriever Rescue of New Jersey.

J. Mark Mutter received his BA from Rutgers University and JD from Western New England College of Law. An attorney-at-law in Toms River, he is a former Dover Township mayor and township committee member and current municipal clerk and township historian. He was chairman of the Dover Township 225th Anniversary Commission and is current chairman of the Toms River Semiquincentennial Commission, as well as adjunct professor at Ocean County College, member of the Ocean County, Sussex County; Sandyston and Walpack Historical Societies and a former member and chairman of the New Jersey Historic Sites Council.

Diana B. Newman holds BS degrees in nursing and music. She has taught in New York and Ohio, where she received national recognition for developing an educational program. As a former member of the 5th Ohio Light Artillery and 6th New York Independent Battery, she represented women who, disguised as men, fought as Civil War soldiers. She is a member of the Camp Olden Civil War Round Table, a volunteer docent at the National Guard Militia Museum of New Jersey in Sea Girt, and, with Robert Silverman, presents Civil War living history programs to organizations in New Jersey.

Gilbert "Skip" Riddle received his BA degree in history from Wilkes University, Wilkes-Barre, Pa. He currently resides in Greenville, NC and is the author of a number of articles and presentations on Civil War history and the use of genealogy as a historical research tool. He has compiled extensive material on the 9th New Jersey Infantry at the battle of New Bern and the history of the 8th New Jersey Infantry, a unit in which his ancestor served. He has made numerous presentations to Civil War Round Tables in New Jersey and North Carolina as well as Sons of Union and Confederate Veterans Chapters and is a New Bern Battlefield Guide and member of the New Bern Historical Society.

Robert L. Silverman received his BS in aerospace engineering and MS in mechanical engineering from Syracuse University. After serving as an army officer, he pursued a career as a research engineer, receiving three US patents. He is a former member of the of the 5th Ohio Light Artillery and 6th New York Independent Battery, a member of the Camp Olden Civil War Round Table, a volunteer docent at the National Guard Militia Museum of New Jersey in Sea Girt, and, with Diana Newman, presents Civil War living history programs to organizations in New Jersey.

Jim Stephens is a native of the Jersey Shore, holds a BA in American History from Montclair State University and an MA in American History from Monmouth University. He has been employed at the Historic Cold Spring Village living history museum, Cape May, New Jersey, since February 2001 and currently serves as the museum's Deputy Director and Education and Interpretation Coordinator

S. Thomas Summers is a teacher of literature and writing at Wayne Hills High School in Wayne, New Jersey and an adjunct writing professor at New Jersey's Passaic County Community College. He has authored two poetry chapbooks and has had his poems published widely in respected literary journals and reviews. Summers is currently working on a full length poetry manuscript titled *Private Hercules McGraw: Poems of the American Civil War*. He lives in Northern New Jersey with his wife Laura and his children, Reanna and Garrett. He blogs at www.thelintinmypocket.wordpress.com.

Joseph A. Truglio is a retired motion picture film technician and lifelong student of the American Civil War. He is a member of the New Jersey Civil War Heritage Association and its 150th Anniversary Committee, as well as several Civil War Round Tables and is currently president of the Phil Kearny Civil War Round Table, in Wayne, New Jersey.

John Zinn received his BA and MBA degrees from Rutgers University and served as an army officer in the Vietnam War. He is currently the chairman of the 150th Anniversary Committee of the New Jersey Civil War Heritage Association and the chairman of the board of the New Jersey Historical Society. He is the author of *The Mutinous Regiment: The Thirty-third New Jersey in the Civil War*, and (with Paul Zinn) *The Major League Pennant Races of 1916: The Most Maddening Baseball Melee in History*.

Bibliography

Books and Pamphlets

Aiken, George, ed. *The Great Locomotive Chase: As Told by the Men Who Made it Happen*. Gatlinburg, TN: Historic Press, 1993.

American Freedman's Union. *The American Freedman, Volume 2*. New York: American Freedman's Union Commission, 1866.

Austin, Anne L. *The Woolsey Sisters of New York*. Philadelphia: American Philosophical Society, 1971.

Baker, Lafayette. *Authentic Stories of Spies, Traitors and Conspirators from the American Secret Service During the Civil War*. Philadelphia: John E. Potter & Company, 1894.

Barthel, Thomas. *Abner Doubleday: A Civil War Biography*. Jefferson, NC: McFarland & Co., 2010.

Bazelon, Bruce, and William McGuinn. *Directory of American Military Goods Dealers and Makers, 1785-1915*. Manassas, VA: Authors, 1999.

Berlin, Ira. *Freedom, Volume 2 Series 1: The Wartime Genesis of Free Labor: The Upper South: A Documentary History of Emancipation, 1861-1867*. New York: Cambridge University Press, 1993.

Bilby, Joseph G. *Freedom to All: New Jersey's African American Soldiers in the Civil War*. Hightstown, NJ: Longstreet House, 2011.

_____ and William C. Goble. *Remember You Are Jerseymen! A Military History of New Jersey's Troops in the Civil War*. Hightstown, NJ: Longstreet House, 1998.

_____ and Harry Ziegler. *Asbury Park: A Brief History*. Charleston, SC: The History Press, 2009.

Brockett, Linus P. and Mary C. Vaughn. *Women's Work in the Civil War: A Record of Heroism, Patriotism and Patience*. Philadelphia: Ziegler, McCurdy & Co., 1867.

Carpenter, Daniel Hoagland. *History and Genealogy of the Carpenter Family in America, From the Settlement at Providence, R. I., 1637 to 1901*. Jamaica, NY: The Marion Press, 1901.

Carroll, John M. *The Custer Autograph Album.* College Station, TX: The Early West, 1994.

Church, William C. *The Life of John Ericsson.* London: Sampson, Low, Marston, Searle & Rivington, 1890.

Clark, Henry. *The Medical Men of New Jersey in Essex District from 1666* to 1866. Newark, NJ: Essex District Medical Society, 1867.

Cook, Robert J. *Troubled Commemoration: The American Civil War Centennial, 1961-1965.* Baton Rouge, LA: LSU Press, 2007.

Cunningham, John T. *New Jersey: America's Main Road.* Garden City, NY: Doubleday & Co., 1966.

_____. *New Jersey: A Mirror on America.* Andover, NJ: Afton Publishing, 2006.

_____. *Railroads in New Jersey: The Formative Years.* Andover, NJ: Afton, 1997

Dorwart, Jeffrey M. *Cape May County New Jersey: The Making of an American Resort Community.* New Brunswick, NJ: Rutgers University Press, 1992.

Drake, J. Madison. *The History of the Ninth New Jersey Veteran Volunteers.* Elizabeth, NJ: Journal Printing House, 1889.

_____. *Fast and Loose in Dixie: An Unprejudiced Narrative of Personal Experience as a Prisoner of War at Libby, Macon, Savannah and Charleston.* New York: Authors' Publishing, 1880.

_____. *Historical Sketches of the Revolutionary and Civil Wars.* New York: Webster Press, 1908.

Eckert, Edward K. *Fiction Distorting Fact: Prison Life, Annotated by Jefferson Davis.* Macon: GA: Mercer University Press, 1988.

Eckhardt, Charles and Robert MacAvoy. *Our Brothers Gone Before* (2 vols.). Hightstown, NJ: Longstreet House, 2006.

Ellis, L. Ethan. *Steps in a Journey Toward Understanding: Activities of the New Jersey Civil War Centennial Commission in 1961 at Trenton, Charleston and Salem Church.* Trenton, NJ: State of New Jersey, 1961.

English, David C. M.D, ed. *Journal of the Medical Society of New Jersey - Volume XIII.* New Brunswick, NJ, 1916

Everts, Herman. *A Complete and Comprehensive History of the Ninth Regiment, NJ Vols. Infantry. From its First Organization to its Final Muster Out.* Newark, NJ: A. Stephen Holbrook, Printer, 1865.

Faust, Drew Gilpin. *This Republic of Suffering: Death and the American Civil War.* New York: Alfred A. Knopf, 2008.

Flayderman, Norm. *Flayderman's Guide to Antique American Firearms and their Values.* Iola, WI: Gun Digest Books, 2007 edition.

Foster, John Y. *New Jersey and the Rebellion: A History of the Services of the Troops and People of New Jersey in Aid of the Union Cause.* Newark, NJ: Dennis & Company, 1868.

Frost, Lawrence. *Custer Legends.* Madison, WI: Popular Press, 1981

Fry, James B. *The Conkling and Blaine-Fry Controversy in 1866.* A. G. Sherwood: New York, 1893.

Gaines, W. Craig. *Encyclopedia of Civil War Shipwrecks.* Baton Rouge, LA: LSU Press, 2008.

Genovese, Eugene D. *Roll, Jordan, Roll: The World the Slaves Made.* New York: Vintage Books, 1976.

Gillette, William. *Jersey Blue: Civil War Politics in New Jersey, 1854-1865.* New Brunswick, NJ: Rutgers University Press, 1994.

Hageman, John Frelinghuysen. *History of Princeton and its Institutions* (2 vols). Philadelphia: J. B. Lippincott, 1879.

Hatch, Thom. *The Custer Companion: A Comprehensive Guide to the Life of George Armstrong Custer and the Plains Indian Wars.* Mechanicsburg, PA: Stackpole, 2002.

Haynes, Martin A. *History of the Second Regiment, New Hampshire Volunteers: Its Camps, Marches and Battles.* Manchester, NH: Charles Livingston, 1865.

Heroux, Jennifer and Stuart C. Mobray, eds. *Civil War Arms Makers and their Contracts: A Facsimile Reprint of the Report by the Commission on Ordnance and Ordnance Stores, 1862.* Lincoln, RI: Andrew Mobray, 1998.

Hall, John F. *The Daily Union History of Atlantic City and County, New Jersey: Containing Sketches of the Past and Present of Atlantic City and County.* Atlantic City, NJ: Daily Union Printing Company, 1900.

Hughes, William E. *U. S. General Hospital at Beverly, New Jersey, 1864-1865.* Stratford, NJ: privately published, 2009.

Jackson, William J. *New Jerseyans in the Civil War: For Union and Liberty.* New Brunswick, NJ: Rutgers University Press, 2006.

Jeffrey, William H. *Richmond Prisons, 1861-1862.* St. Johnsbury, VT: The Republican Press, 1893.

Johnson, Nelson. *Boardwalk Empire.* Medford, NJ: Plexus Publishing, 2002.

Johnson, William J. *Abraham Lincoln, The Christian.* New York: Eaton & Mains, 1915.

Kennedy, Steele Mabon, ed. *The New Jersey Almanac, 1964-1965.* Upper Montclair, NJ: New Jersey Almanac Inc., 1963.

Kline, Michael J. *The Baltimore Plot: The First Conspiracy to Assassinate Abraham Lincoln.* Yardley, PA: Westholme Publishing, 2008.

Korn, Bertram W. *American Jewry in the Civil War.* New York: Jewish Publications Society, 2001.

Lewis, A. S. ed. *My Dear Parents: The Civil War as Seen by an English Union Soldier, James Horrocks.* NY: Harcourt, Brace Jovanovitch, 1982.

Longacre, Edward G. *To Gettysburg and Beyond: The Twelfth New Jersey Volunteer Infantry , II Army Corps, Army of the Potomac, 1862-1865.* Hightstown, NJ: Longstreet House, 1992.

Lurie, Maxine N. and Marc Mappen. *Encyclopedia of New Jersey.* New Brunswick, NJ: Rutgers University Press, 1994.

Marbaker, Thomas. *History of the Eleventh New Jersey Volunteers.* Hightstown, NJ: Longstreet House, 1990. (Reprint of 1898 edition)

Martin, David G., ed. *The Monocacy Regiment: A Commemorative History of the Fourteenth New Jersey in the Civil War, 1862-1865.* Hightstown, NJ: Longstreet House, 1987.

_____. *Camp Vredenburg in the Civil War.* Hightstown, NJ: Longstreet House, 1993.

Martin, Louis. *Beaufort County Heroes 1861-1865.* [n.p.], 2003.

Martin, Samuel. *Kill Cavalry: Sherman's Merchant of Terror: The Life of Union General Hugh Judson Kilpatrick.* Teaneck, NJ: Fairleigh Dickinson University Press, 1996.

McAfee, Michael J. *Zouaves: The First and the Bravest.* Gettysburg, PA: Thomas Publications, 1996.

McCaulay, John D. *Civil War Pistols.* Lincoln, RI: Andrew Mobray Publishers, 1992.

McConnell, Stuart. *Glorious Contentment: The Grand Army of the Republic, 1865-1900.* University of North Carolina Press, 1997.

Miers, Earl Schenck. *New Jersey in the Year of the Proclamation - an Address by Earl Schenck Miers.* New Brunswick, NJ: New Brunswick Historical Club, 1963.

_____. *New Jersey in the Civil War.* Princeton, NJ: D. Van Nostrand Co., 1964.

Miller, Pauline. *Ocean County: Four Centuries in the Making.* Toms River, NJ: Ocean County Cultural and Heritage Commission, 2000.

Mills, W. Jay. *Historic Houses of New Jersey.* Philadelphia: JB Lippincott Company, 1902.

Moore, Frank. *Women of the War: Their Heroism and Self Sacrifice.* Hartford, CT: S. S. Scranton & Co., 1866.

Murdock, Eugene C. *Patriotism Limited: The Civil War Draft and the Bounty System.* Kent, OH: Kent State University Press, 1967.

New York State Civil War Centennial Commission. *Monitor Centennial Issue, New York State and the Civil War.* Albany, NY: 1962.

Nunn, J. Harold. *The Story of Hackettstown, New Jersey 1754-1955.* Hackettstown, NJ: Hackettstown Bank, 1956.

Nutter, Waldo E. *Manhattan Firearms.* Harrisburg, PA: Stackpole Company, 1958.

Olmstead, Edwin, Wayne E. Stark and Spencer C. Tucker. *The Big Guns: Civil War Siege, Seacoast and Naval Cannons.* Bloomfield, ONT: Museum Restoration Service,1997.

Orr, John W. Jr. *"Reflections from the Shrine": An Anecdotal History of Hightstown and East Windsor.* Hightstown, NJ: Longstreet House, 1998.

Richards, Jay C. and Nancy Smith. *Officers and Men of Warren County in the Civil War.* Phillipsburg, NJ: Authors, 2005.

Ripley, Warren. *Artillery and Ammunition of the Civil War*. New York, NY: Promontory Press, 1970.

Rizzo, Dennis. *Parallel Communities: The Underground Railroad in South Jersey*. Charleston, SC: The History Press, 2008.

Robertson, James I. *The Civil War Letters of General Robert McAllister*. New Brunswick, NJ: Rutgers University Press, 1965.

Rogers Locomotive. *Locomotives and Locomotive Building/Origin and Growth of the Rogers Locomotive and Machine Works, Paterson, New Jersey: From 1831 to 1886*. New York: Wm. S Gottsberger, 1886.

Rose, Willie Lee. *Rehearsal for Reconstruction: The Port Royal Experiment*. New York: Oxford University Press, 1964.

Rusling, James Fowler. *Men and Things I Saw in Civil War Days*. New York: Curtis and Jenning, 1899.

Semmes, Raphael. *Memoirs of Service Afloat During The War Between The States*. Baltimore, MD: Kelly Piot & Company, 1869.

Scherzer, Carl B. *Early Jewish History in Morristown*. Morristown, NJ: Author, 1977.

Siegel, Alan A. *For the Glory of the Union: Myth, Reality and the Media in Civil War New Jersey*. Teaneck, NJ: Fairleigh Dickinson University Press, 1984.

Snell, James P. *History of Sussex and Warren Counties New Jersey with Illustrations and Biographical Sketches of Prominent Men and Pioneers*. Philadelphia: Everts & Peck. 1881.

Spann, Edward K. *Gotham at War: New York City, 1860-1865*. Wilmington, DE: Scholarly Resources, 2002.

State of New Jersey. *Quartermaster General Reports, 1860-1905*. Trenton, NJ, 1861-1906.

State of New Jersey Monument Commission. *New Jersey's Ninth Regiment, 1861-1905. Report of the New Jersey State Commission for Erection of the Monument to the Ninth New Jersey Volunteers at New Bern, North Carolina. Dedication at the National Cemetery in New Bern, North Carolina May 18, 1905*. Trenton: State of New Jersey,1905.

State of New Jersey Civil War Centennial Commission. *Special Joint Session of NJ Senate & General Assembly - Commemorating the 100th Anniversary of Abraham Lincoln's Historic Appearance Before the Legislature February 21, 1861.* Trenton, NJ: State of New Jersey, 1961.

_____. *Second Annual American History Workshop presented by New Jersey Civil War Centennial Commission Saturday, December 8, 1962.* New Brunswick, NJ: Rutgers University Press, 1962.

_____. *Rededication Program - Honoring the Memory of the Gallant New Jersey Men Who Fought in the Battles of Salem Church, The Wilderness and Spotsylvania Court House.* Trenton, State of NJ, 1961.

_____. *New Jersey in the Civil War and Civil War Facts Compiled by NJ Civil War Centennial Commission.* Trenton, State of New Jersey, 1961.

Still, William N. *Iron Afloat: The Story of the Confederate Armorclads.* Columbia, SC: University of South Carolina Press (reprint), 1988.

Styple, William B. and John J. Fitzpatrick, ed. *The Andersonville Diary and Memoirs of Charles Hopkins.* Kearny, NJ: Belle Grove Publishing, 1988.

Styple, William B., ed. *Tell Me of Lincoln: Memories of Abraham Lincoln, the Civil War & Life in Old New York* by "James E. Kelly." Kearny, NJ: Belle Grove Publishing, 2009.

Sutherland, Robert Q. and R. L. Wilson. *The Book of Colt Firearms.* Kansas City, MO: Robert Q. Sutherland, 1971.

Swinton, William, *History of the Seventh Regiment, National Guard, State of New York, in the War of the Rebellion.* New York: Fields, Osgood & Co., 1870.

Switala, William J. *Underground Railroad in New York and New Jersey.* Mechanicsburg, PA: Stackpole, 2006.

Tarshish, Allan. *Rise of American Judaism: A History of American Jewish life from 1848 to 1881.* New York: Hebrew Union College, 1938.

Temple, Brian. *The Union Prison at Fort Delaware: A Perfect Hell on Earth.* Jefferson, NC: McFarland Publishing, 2003.

The Lincoln Monument in Memory of Scottish-American Soldiers. Edinburgh: William Blackwood and Sons, 1893.

The Transactions of the American Medical Association - Volume XIX. AMA: Philadelphia: 1868.

Todd, Frederick P. *American Military Equipage, 1851-1872.* Rutland, MA: Company of Military Historians, 1977.

Tuttle, Brad R. *How Newark Became Newark*: *The Rise, Fall and Rebirth of an American City.* New Brunswick, NJ: Rutgers University Press, 2009.

United States Civil War Centennial Commission. *Guide for the Observance of the Centennial of the Civil War.* Washington, DC, 1959.

Warner, Ezra J. *Generals in Gray: Lives of the Confederate Commanders.* Baton Rouge, LA: LSU Press, 1959.

Welles, Gideon. *Diary of Gideon Welles: Secretary of the Navy Under Lincoln and Johnson Vol. I.* New York: Houghton Mifflin, 1911.

Winfield, Charles F. *History of the County of Hudson, New Jersey, From its Earliest Settlement to the Present Time.* New York: Kennard and Hay, 1874.

Wolff, Daniel. *4th of July, Asbury Park: A History of the Promised Land.* New York: Bloomsbury, 2005.

Wolf, Simon and Louis Edward Levy. *The American Jew as Patriot, Soldier and Civilian.* Philadelphia: Levytype Company, 1895.

Woodward E.M., and John F. Hageman. *History of Burlington and Mercer Counties, NJ.* Philadelphia: Everts & Peck, 1883.

Wright, Giles R. *Afro-Americans in New Jersey: A Short History.* Trenton: New Jersey Historical Commission, 1988.

Zall, P. M. *Abe Lincoln Laughing: Humorous Anecdotes from Original Sources by and about Abraham Lincoln.* Berkeley, CA: University of California Press, 1982.

Zinn, John. *The Mutinous Regiment: The Thirty Third New Jersey in the Civil War.* Jefferson, NC: McFarland & Co., 2005.

Articles:

Bilby, Joseph. "Scoundrels from New York and Philadelphia: A Look at New Jersey's Zouave Regiments." *Military Images Magazine* Vol. X, No. 2, September-October, 1988.

Kuhl, John. "Camp Flemington, 1863." *Hunterdon County Historical Newsletter,* v. 21, no. 3.

Martin, David. "Hightstown in the Civil War." *Princeton (NJ) Recollector.* Vol. 6, No. 7 (April 1981).

Stryker, William S. "The 'Swamp Angel.'" *Battles and Leaders of the Civil War.* New York: The Century Company, 1888. Vol. 4.

Sturcke, Roger D. and Michael J. MacAfee. "33rd Regiment, New Jersey Volunteer Infantry, '2nd Zouaves.'" *Military Collector and Historian*, vol. 31, no. 3.

Sturcke, Roger D. and Michael J. Winey and Earle J. Coates. "35th New Jersey Volunteer Infantry Regiment, (Cladek's Zouaves)," *Military Collector and Historian.* vol. 28, no. 3.

Robinson, Thomas A. "Keystone Crafts Large Civil War Memorial Replacement." *Elberton Graniteer,* Vol. 46, No. 1, Spring 2002.

Welles, Gideon. "The First Ironclad." Philadelphia *Weekly Times Annals of the War,* Vol. 1, No. 1, March 3, 1877.

Newspapers and Periodicals

American Freedman
Cape May *Ocean Wave*
Concord *New Hampshire Patriot*
Concord, New Hampshire, *Daily Independent Democrat*
Frank Leslie's Illustrated Newspaper
Harper's Weekly
Hightstown *Gazette*
Hunterdon *Democrat*
Hunterdon *Gazette*
Hunterdon *Republican*
Illustrated Times of London
Iola (Iowa) *Register*
Jersey City *American Standard*
Jersey City *Courier*
Lambertville (NJ) *Beacon*
Macon (GA) *Telegraph*
Morristown *Record*
Newark Journal
Newark Daily Advertiser
Newark *Daily Mercury*
Newark News
Newark *Star Ledger*
New Brunswick *Times*
Newton *Sussex Register*
New York Clipper
New York *Herald*
New York *Reformer*
New York Times
New York *Tribune*
Paterson *Press*
Raleigh (NC) *News and Observer*
Somerset *Messenger Gazette*
Somerset (NJ) *Democrat*
Toms River *Ocean Emblem*
The Illustrated Times of London
Trentonian
Trenton *Monitor*
Trenton *True American*
Warren *Reporter*
Washington (NC) *Daily News*
Washington Post
Woodbury *Constitution*

Unpublished Material:

Harding, Edward, "Confederate Ancestors of Edward Harding: The War of Southern Independence (1861-1865)."

Kinney, Jonathan D. "Swindlers, Pimps and Vagabonds: New Jersey's Civil War Bounty Jumpers" MA Thesis, William Paterson University, 2004.

Riddle, Gilbert V., "The 9th N.J. Volunteer Infantry in the Civil War:Lore of the 9th N.J."

Tersigni, Terry W., "No Strangers in Blood: A Genealogical History of the Families that Settled the Musconetcong Valley in New Jersey."

Manuscripts

Camden County Historical Society
Davis Papers

Hunterdon County Historical Society
William E. Haver Papers

John Kuhl Collection
Dayton Flint letters
John Laughton letters

Metro West Historical Society
Deetlebach Letters

New Jersey Historical Society
Marcus Ward papers, NJHS, Newark, NJ
Mindil papers, NJHS, Newark, NJ
William James Evans papers

National Archives and Records Administration
Various soldier service and pension records.

National Guard Militia Museum of New Jersey
Kinsey family papers

New Jersey State Archives
New Jersey Civil War Centennial Commission papers NJ State Archives

Stanford University Library
Edward Martindale papers

Western Reserve Historical Society, Cleveland, Ohio
William Lloyd Papers

Online Sources
bit.ly/GenGracie
bit.ly/Newarkfirearm
bit.ly/EliasWright
bit.ly/LincolnClassRoom
bit.ly/Van_Zant
bit.ly/HCHistory
bit.ly/Margerum
bit.ly/EWrightGrave

Miscellaneous
Historic Cold Spring Village (Cape May) Interpretive Manuals
Interview with Kathryn Carlson
Interview with Edward Harding
Interview with Charles Prestopine
Interview with Billy Van Zandt
Interview with Bob Murgittroyd

Index

Four score and seven years ago our fathers brought forth on this continent, a new nation, conceived in Liberty, and dedicated to the proposition that all men are created equal.

Now we are engaged in a great civil war, testing whether that nation, or any nation so conceived and so dedicated, can long endure. We are met on a great battle-field of that war. We have come to dedicate a portion of that field, as a final resting place for those who here gave their lives that that nation might live. It is altogether fitting and proper that we should do this.

But, in a larger sense, we can not dedicate -- we can not consecrate -- we can not hallow -- this ground. The brave men, living and dead, who struggled here, have consecrated it, far above our poor power to add or detract. The world will little note, nor long remember what we say here, but it can never forget what they did here. It is for us the living, rather, to be dedicated here to the unfinished work which they who fought here have thus far so nobly advanced. It is rather for us to be here dedicated to the great task remaining before us -- that from these honored dead we take increased devotion to that cause for which they gave the last full measure of devotion -- that we here highly resolve that these dead shall not have died in vain -- that this nation, under God, shall have a new birth of freedom -- and that government of the people, by the people, for the people, shall not perish from the earth.

New Jersey Plot at Gettysburg National Cemetery, Remembrance Day, 2010 (Arthur Green)